RECONCILED FROM ABORTION'S CHAINS

SHARON MCFEE

Ark House Press
PO Box 1722, Port Orchard, WA 98366 USA
PO Box 1321, Mona Vale NSW 1660 Australia
PO Box 318 334, West Harbour, Auckland 0661 New Zealand
arkhousepress.com

Some names and identifying details have been changed to protect the privacy of individuals.

Cataloguing in Publication Data:
Title: Reconciled from Abortion's Chains
ISBN: 978-0-6488873-2-4 (pbk)
Other Authors/Contributors: McFee, Sharon

Design by initiateagency.com

CONTENTS

ACKNOWLEDGEMENTS

I DEDICATE THIS BOOK FIRST and foremost to my Lord and Saviour Jesus Christ, without whom this book would never have been written. He has turned my life from pain to salvation, from challenge to triumph, and from defeat to victory! To my God-given husband Peter, who has given me permission to share these intimate details; to my daughters Janessa and Kayley, who patiently collated the book together; to my daughter-in-law Hayley, who quietly prayed for me and the outcome of the book; to my three sons, and to all my extended family and friends.

I also thank these people who encouraged me to write this book and believed that this was God's will for me. They are: my friend Lesley who introduced me to a greater awareness of the Holy Spirit; the Phillip Island Baptist Church, Victoria, who prayed for the book during church; Andy and Nicole's Bible study group who laid hands on me and prayed; my sister Roslyn who had a confirming dream one night; the Harvest Life Church in Emerald, Queensland; and Carol for her comments and the use of her printer. And thanks goes to my dear friend Felicity who was willing and able to go through and edit my book with me. Lois, I especially would like to thank you for the polishing of my book and for giving me the chance to bounce my thoughts and ideas off you, for all the hard work you have put into my book, and to my lifelong friend Robyn Swift who was led to do an editing and proofreading course which turned out to be of enormous benefit to me at the exact right time. Many thanks for fleshing out the conversations.

These people encouraged God's vision He has given to me to minister to women and to see them healed, delivered, and set free. All to the glory of God!

THE BEGINNING OF THE END

What have I done? I thought as intense pain hit me as my stomach cramped yet again. I lay on the bed, slowly realising the enormous consequences which were now beginning to play out from the choice I had made. The pain was relentless – not just the physical pain but the heavy weight of emotional pain I now bore –guilt!

The doctor had left the room to attend to other patients; I was all alone, not even a nurse to comfort and support me. The doctor came back and checked on me; I was in a bad way. He led me to a back room in the surgery. Hours later, I hadn't recovered as quickly as the doctor expected. He was concerned for me no doubt because of the negative ramifications to his professional name and practice. (It was illegal for abortions to be performed in Queensland.)

I made a vow that day: I would never find myself in this situation ever again! I finally managed to get up off the bed, weak and frightened, and quickly exited his surgery. Sliding myself gingerly into my car, I numbly made my way back home, wincing in pain as I drove over the railway line.

Home again, alone. My family were due back the next day from their annual holidays.

Another piercing pain overtook me. I lay still on my bed for a few seconds, trying to control my breathing, and then, flung the blankets off and ran to the toilet. Just making it, I felt the unwanted lifeless embryo expel itself out of my body. I looked down in horror at the jelly-like mass. The nightmare haunted me. What I did not realise at that time was that a part of me died that day. After all, this was flesh of my flesh.

For all have sinned, and come short of
the glory of God. (Rom. 3: 23)

CHAPTER 1

Behold! I have been standing at the door and I am knocking: if someone would hear My voice and would open the door, then I will enter to him and I will dine with him and he with Me. (Rev. 3: 20)

My Australian father married my New Zealand-born mother in Auckland, New Zealand. Due to the low economical climate, they moved to Darwin, Australia, where it was rumoured jobs were a dime a dozen, but jobs were not that easy to get.

'Ken!' my mother cried out as her waters broke. Dad rushed into the bedroom to see what the commotion was all about. 'We need to go to the hospital. I think I had a contraction.' Mum panicked. She still had five weeks to go before I was due.

Four hours later, I arrived kicking and screaming into the world, weighing five pounds six ounces.

A few months later, plans were being made to move to Brisbane, on the east coast of Australia, where they were offered a job running a corner store.

'It will be easier on Sharon to fly,' my father said.

'You know I hate flying,' my mother replied. 'I'll take the bus.'

After much deliberation, they came to a decision: I was to fly with my father, and then we would meet my mother at the bus station. That was my first ever plane trip, and definitely not my last.

In Brisbane, Mum and Dad met up with some people who invited them to a Christian meeting.

'What can we lose by going?' Mum said. 'We can always leave if we aren't happy with the meeting. I don't know, you should know how they try to manipulate you into believing things that are not true. Jesus Christ alive? How can a meeting prove Jesus is alive? It will take more than that to make me believe, that's for sure.'

'We'll sit at the back and leave as soon as it's over. Really what can we lose?' Mum repeated. She was curious and wanted to find out for herself.

The meeting was held in a small hall down the road from where we lived. They entered the hall with trepidation and sat in the last row of seats by the back door.

'Hi, you decided to come? I am so glad you did. Let me introduce you to these people down the front,' a middle-aged man said as he held out his hand to my father.

'Thanks, but maybe after the meeting. We will stay here just in case Sharon wakes, we don't want her screaming through the meeting.'

'Ok, I'll see you later then.' He moved off to speak to another couple who had walked through the door.

The meeting was much more than either of them had expected. Everything said, brought peace to their hearts; they were so enthralled that when the speaker asked for people to come to the front and give their lives to the Lord, they willingly went up.

Their lives changed; God is alive; He knows them and died for them. He is real – so much so that when the suggestion for Dad to study Accountancy at the Bible College was made, they accepted and moved to Cooranbong in New South Wales.

Rose, my sister, was born in Cooranbong Hospital.

Once the course was finished, we moved to Adelaide, where my parents tried to settle, but Mum was restless no matter where we lived.

I could feel myself falling and then hit the hard lino floor; pain shot up through my small body, and I screamed.

The ship was swaying to and fro. Our cabin consisted of a bunk bed; I slept on top, Rose on the bottom, and a double bed where mum and dad slept. We were lucky to have our own bathroom which was small even to my little eyes.

'What's the matter, Sharon?' Mum woke up startled. 'Did you fall out of the bunk?' Mum flung off her blankets, climbed out of bed, and picked me up off the floor. The pain settled to a dull ache, but I still cried. 'You can sleep with me. Shhh, it's all right. There now go to sleep.' My mother folded me in her arms after pulling the blankets over us.

In the morning, Mum and Dad packed up. We then traipsed up to the dining room for breakfast. As the ship approached the wharf at Auckland, New Zealand, I looked up to Rose who was in Mum's arms, giggling, pointing to the mountains. 'Look! Can you see those funny hills?' This was an adventure. Rose tried to wriggle out of Mum's arms. 'Hills! Hills!' she said pointing into the distance.

The ship docked, and we watched as people disembarked. I tried to run towards the gangway. Dad held me back. 'Don't be so impatient. There is plenty of time. We have to wait for the others to leave.'

'Look at the funny skirts on those people, Mum.' I giggled excitedly, pointing to the women on the wharf. They wore traditional Maori piupiu skirts 'Can we wear skirts like that too?'

'One day you can, but not now,' Dad answered while guiding me down the ramp. We caught a taxi; Rose and I were jumping on the back seat trying to see all the people, cars, and hills.

'Sit still, girls!' Dad scolded us, 'You're distracting the driver. There's plenty of time to look around once we get to our new home.'

Our home was an old wooden house Mum and Dad rented.

A scream came from the dining room. 'It's a mouse!' One of Mum's pet hates was mice. 'I can't wait until we move out of this horrible house into the new one,' Mum cried out in frustration.

'For goodness sake, it's only a mouse!' Dad yelled at Mum while she was jumping fearfully from one leg to the other. 'How did you cope before when there was a mouse plague?'

'I have never lived where there was a plague. And if I had known there was one here, I wouldn't have come!' Mum screamed back at Dad.

'You're frightening the girls. For goodness' sake, settle down. The last thing I need is three screaming girls.' He walked out shaking his head.

A few weeks later, we moved into our new home. Mum was so happy; she looked as if she was going to jump for joy. 'Isn't this wonderful, our own home?' Mum looked around the big lounge room and then walked down a small hallway into another room. 'And this will be your room, girls. It's painted pink for my beautiful little girls, and look, you even have a shelf each to put your books on.' We ran behind her to explore the house. Our room was the biggest room I had seen for a bedroom, pink walls with white trimmings and white doors into the wardrobe.

'Coming through, girls, quick, out the way, or you will get run over.' Dad and a friend were struggling with a bed. 'Where do you want it?'

'I think one bed on each side of the room. Then the girls can play in the middle.' Eventually the house was filled with all our belongings, and we gradually settled down to life in New Zealand.

I started school about the same time as we moved in. Mum took Rose and me to school. I had never been away from Mum even for a day, so when she said she was leaving, I grabbed onto her leg and wouldn't let go. 'Don't leave me here, Mum,' I cried desperately as she tried to untwine my fingers wrapped around leg. 'Sharon, don't be ridiculous,' Mum responded. 'Now, let go. This is school. You have to stay here.'

'No, I want to go with you!' I cried, tears streaming down my face. 'Need some help here?' a woman said as she walked over to us smiling. 'It seems to be a common problem today. Is your name Sharon? I'm Miss Rhodes, your teacher.' She bent down so she could see me. 'I would be very unhappy to see you go. How would you like to come with me and see where you will be sitting? Paula will be sitting next to you. Come and meet her too.'

She took hold of my hand as Mum peeled it off her leg. Miss Rhodes turned me around so I could see the other children; when I turned back, Mum and Rose had gone. I was devastated. I didn't stop crying for ages. Finally, I looked around at my new surroundings and noticed the other kids; Paula was holding my hand.

I adapted and soon won an award for something or other; I chose from a range of prizes offered and joyfully selected an Elvis Presley book. Mum, Rose, and I loved Elvis and would go to the movies to see him or West Side Story. My Mum would laugh so loud, I'd slink underneath my seat in embarrassment.

My mother was not noted for her cooking, and I well remember the burnt toast and stews which I still love. I felt secure and loved in my little world. Unbeknown to me my world was about to change.

My mother had been very close to her father while growing up, but he walked out on his daughter and wife unexpectedly, leaving her with her mother who was distant. When her mother remarried, she was sent to a boarding school.

Very little was said about my mother's past and neither was it encouraged. She would often say, 'And that is the last I will say about that.' And the subject was never mentioned again.

Dad had a good job as an accountant in a gas company, but bills had to be paid, so Mum found a job working in a milk bar to help out financially.

One night, Rose and I were going to sleep when we heard yelling coming from my parents' room. 'Who's that?' Rose asked as she sat up in her bed, turning to look at me. 'Shh,' I said putting my pointer finger to my mouth to indicate to Rose to be quiet. Muffled sounds came from my parent's bedroom and then shouting again. 'I'm scared. Can I come in bed with you?' Rose jumped off her bed and ran into mine. We hugged each other listening. I had never felt so scared. Rose was shaking and then started to cry. 'It's Mum and Dad. They are having an argument. It will be all right Rose, shh,' I said, comforting Rose while trying to control my own fears.

Over the next few weeks, Rose and I were woken to Mum and Dad's shouting. Then one night, Mum moved into the spare room. Not long after, Dad moved into a flat close by.

Rose and I felt confused, having no understanding of what was happening; our parents didn't think to explain. I was only seven at the time, and life had changed.

Mum had to work long hours, and over a period of twelve months, we stayed at three different neighbours after school; I detested it because each family had different sets of rules. We were often told to go outside, so we made our own fun.

'Get down from there!' Rose yelled at me one day. 'Oh, Rose, watch me fly!' I was on the shed roof looking down, watching Rose and Allen run towards the shed. It was good being so high; life seemed peaceful; everything looked smaller on the ground; the sky felt close; I lifted my arms up and believed I could touch the sky; at the same time, I felt I could control everything. If I could fly, I would be free to go anywhere I wanted and no one could stop me. All I had to do was jump and spread my arms. The thought gave me great pleasure. My imagination went rife. 'Sharon, it's too far up, you'll get hurt.' Rose was always the sensible one. 'Come down now. I'm scared!'

'Don't be silly. All I want to do is see if I can fly,' I shouted. 'Sharon, don't do it.' Allen, our neighbour's son, agreed.

I looked at their faces; Rose had tears in her eyes, Allen's showed fear. Why did they have to spoil my attempt to fly? I did as they suggested and climbed down feeling let down and was angry, not only with them, but myself for not doing what I wanted, even to the detriment of what could have happened if I did.

At another time, I was climbing a high cedar pine tree with the boys until I got something in my eye. I ran home and called Mum at work. 'Sharon, I can't take you to the doctor's, so you'll need to go yourself,' Mum said over the phone. My immediate reaction was fear; my eye was stinging, tears streamed down my face making it hard for me to see. The thought of going to the doctor's on my own was terrifying. 'Ok,' I mumbled, trying not to cry and replaced the phone on the hook.

I bravely walked down to the doctor's, which was a few streets away, then waited until I was called, and followed him into his room and explained what had happened. He looked into my eye. 'You'll have to go to the hospital. I can't do anything here for you.'

'I don't have any money to get there. What can I do?' I said concerned. *What would Mum say?* He thought for a few minutes. 'Follow me. We'll organise something.' He spoke quietly to the receptionist who then gave me some money which I used to catch the bus.

The bus stop was near the hospital, but I couldn't walk all the way, so I caught a taxi. To my horror, I didn't have enough money after I arrived at the hospital. 'I'll wait until you get out and take you home. Then your parents can pay me.' The taxi driver was wonderful.

I went in and waited until I was called. The sister examined my eye. 'I can't do anything without your parents' consent. You'll have to come back with them.' I was beside myself with worry, and my eye was still painful.

The taxi driver took me home.

I ended up having the operation on my eye.

Mum had struggled as a single parent trying to raise Rose and me while working without extended family support. Dad moved back home, and Mum moved out. My role changed from being a big sister to being a mother figure for Rose.

I comforted myself by caring for my pet fish and the praying mantis insects which clung to the bush out front of our house. I started daydreaming, wondering what it would be like living in their world, pretending I was a praying mantis climbing over the leaves and branches getting higher and higher seeing the world, or just staying in one place as if I was part of a branch invisible to all around. It was my way of escaping from reality.

'Come on, Sharon and Rose, we're going out for awhile. I have a surprise for you,' Dad called out one afternoon while we were playing in the yard. We jumped excitedly into the car and questioned him, 'a surprise' was all he said smiling.

We pulled up at a huge shed. Dad took our hands, and we went into the shed, following lots of other people. My eyes popped open, and my mouth dropped; there were toys everywhere: dolls, cars, boats, prams, fluffy toys, all jam-packed into the shed. 'You can have anything you want, girls,' Dad said waving his arm around. I ran around looking in wonder at all the toys. I chose a beautiful doll called Jane. She had a cord in her back. On pulling the cord, she said, 'I love you, Mummy.' Dad tended to spoil us with toys; needless to say, our spare room was filled knee-deep with them. At the time, I believed I could have anything I liked.

Dad would sometimes take us girls to church. After church, I would pull down books and lay on my tummy looking at the pictures of Jesus with the children crowded around Him. My idea of heaven was running around playing with miniature people without a care in the world. The picture that remained permanently imprinted on my brain was of Jesus gently holding a little lost lamb in His enfolded arms. When I felt circumstances were beyond my control, I believed I was the lost lamb He was carrying. Jesus was there for me.

My dad now struggled as a sole parent without family support, so an SOS was sent across to Brisbane, Australia, where his mother and sister, Betsy, lived. My grandma, short in stature but bold in spirit, had just been recovering from major surgery to remove a portion of her bowel due to cancer. The doctors told her she would not recover from the operation, but upon hearing of our predicament, she summoned all her strength and health and flew over and took care of us. I could not remember meeting her before, but when she arrived, it felt like I had known her all my life; her sacrificial love touched me deeply. She became my role model, my second mother, as I thought of her then, and I gratefully received her love and attention. My grandmother organised my ninth birthday and the first real birthday party I could ever remember. I felt valued and loved. Despite all the changes in my life and the emotional upheaval, I was doing very well at school, showing promising signs of leadership.

Six months went past, and this particular day Dad came into our room. 'Girls, I want you to go with your grandmother to live in Australia. You'll be staying with your Aunty Betsy. I have to stay here in Auckland for a few months longer, but I promise that as soon as I can, I will come over and we will be together again.'

Ros and I cried all the way to the airport. Neither of us wanted to leave Dad behind; even with his promise, we were afraid we would never see him again and felt abandoned!

We flew across to warm Brisbane in sunny Queensland and immediately noticed that the weather was different. 'At long last, you must be Sharon and this must be Rose,' my aunty enthused, 'welcome, come and meet your Uncle Ray, and these boys are your cousins. We have been looking forward to having you stay with us.' She gave us a big hug and then ushered us into the car while still introducing us to her sons as we drove back to her home. 'This is your room. Grandma will be living in the flat out back.' Our room was larger than the one at home. Two of my cousins had given up their bedroom for Rose and me to share. I was relieved to be in the same room as Rose. Rose looked lost and kept looking at me for support. I had to be brave for both of us. We really had only known grandma for six months and now we had an aunt, an uncle, and three cousins in a new country! Well, not really new, but, I was young when I left. Accepting our new family was great, but the loss of both Mum and Dad affected Rose and me more deeply than realised at the time. Through my eyes, life was certainly different in Australia to New Zealand.

August meant it was part-way through the school year and a decision had to be made as to which grades would be suitable for us to go into. I was put into grade 4 and struggled to keep up with the other students as I tried to adapt, especially since the educational levels were so different. Rose was placed into grade 2 but was put down into grade 1 because of the educational gap.

'There he is!' we shouted while jumping up and down with excitement as our father entered the terminal at the Brisbane airport. It had been six months since we left New Zealand, and I had celebrated my tenth birthday in Australia. 'Dad,' we shouted again waving. 'My girls, you look wonderful. I missed you so much.' He hugged us and then hugged his mother. 'It's good to be here at last.' I felt shy not knowing how to react; he held his arms out to Rose and me, and then talked about a woman he had met at his workplace whom he was going to correspond with. We walked out of the airport not totally understanding what our father was talking about, a woman?

Dad bought a house near Aunty Betsy's. Grandma moved in with us and continued to take care of our needs.

Grade 5 was still a struggle as I had not caught up to the educational level. Aunty Betsy tried to help me as she had once been a schoolteacher, while grandma cooked up a storm baking home-made apple pies and jam tarts, and we all realised that I now enjoyed food. I began to gain weight.

During my sixth year at school, grandma's health deteriorated. One day, she called me into her bedroom and said, 'Close the door, Sharon. I want to show you something.' I closed the door behind me not knowing what to expect. Grandma lifted up her blouse revealing the colostomy bag attached to the side of her abdomen. 'I thought it would be helpful for you to understand something about my health.' I recoiled in horror at the unnatural sight of the bag as it dawned on me that my grandmother's health was deteriorating.

Grandma then moved back to Aunty Betsy's place. She suffered a stroke not long after, paralysing her down her right side, which meant that she now required assistance with feeding.

'Hi, Grandma,' I said as I climbed onto her bed and sat next to her. I visited her on my way home from school each day. 'Shall I go on to where I left yesterday? Where were we? Oh yes, John 3,' and I continued to read the Bible aloud while she laid captive listening to every word. By then, she could no longer talk. To see a strong woman like this was so hard, but I wanted all the time I could get to be with her and to bring her a little joy to show her how much I loved her. I had looked up to her as a role model.

My father continued communicating through letters with Lauren who was living in Auckland, New Zealand. They decided to marry. At the time, the law stated that a couple had to be separated for five years before a divorce would be granted. My mother in New Zealand fell pregnant and gave birth to a son – whom we met later when he was eighteen – which granted my parents an early divorce.

My father flew over to New Zealand and on 9 December 1967 married Lauren. Rose and I stayed with Aunty Betsy and didn't attend their wedding due to limited finances.

Within days of my father's marriage, my grandmother passed away. Rose and I were devastated. She was one person who really loved and cared for us. We were able to talk to her in ways we were never able to do with either Mum or Dad. And she listened to everything we had to say, giving us good advice, laughing and joking with us. She was a wonderful Godly woman. Her death left a vacuum in our lives.

I was given the choice of attending my grandmother's funeral or going to the class break-up party. I chose the latter.

In my mind, I had four mothers: my mother (Mum) was naturally my first; then my grandmother took her place being my second; after we moved to Brisbane, my Aunty Betsy took over for a while becoming my third; and then my stepmother (mother) became my fourth. A whole new chapter began in our lives as a blended family. Lauren had been a cooking demonstrator at the gas company where my father had worked, and we were blessed with tasty and nutritious food. Many new rules were introduced which I complied to but inwardly rebelled. Life was again different. I know Dad wanted a mother for us, but his remarrying actually pushed my sister and me away from them, and we now turned to each other for love and support.

Grade 7 was my favourite year, because Mr Magoo, an elderly man affected by polio leaving him with a speech impediment, believed in me. He looked out for all the students in his class who were struggling for whatever reason and encouraged them to reach their greatest potential. He was the best teacher any child could have. My grades gradually improved until they were within the range of my schooling in New Zealand, near the top of the class. I realised that I could do it, I could succeed, I could overcome obstacles and challenges before me; I really could win.

While Mum and Dad were having a lie-in on Sundays, Rose and I would don hats and handbags and check out different churches on our own. We didn't care which church we went to, we just wanted to know God. Eventually we ended up at the Baptist church and joined the Girls Life Brigade which we attended on Friday nights. There was great excitement abuzz at the time because this world-famous evangelist was coming to town, and his name was Billy Graham. A bus was arranged for all of us to go with the youth, and Rose and I gladly joined in. There at the large sports ground at Woolloongabba, a suburb of Brisbane, we heard the most impacting message we had ever heard in our young lives; we were both so overcome with emotion as Billy Graham spoke of how we had all sinned and how we needed to turn away from it to get our lives right. The Bible tells us that we were all born into sin and fall short of the glory of God. This was really hard to comprehend, when, for most people, we think that because we obey the law and do the right thing, we don't sin. What we don't take into consideration is the fact we do things that are not perfect that is, say things to hurt people, get angry when we shouldn't, think thoughts that are not pure, and so we sin in the sight of God. God sent Jesus to pay for all the sins we have done in the past as well as those we will commit in the future.

An altar call was made, and, weeping, I rushed forward with Rose not far behind, and we made a decision to follow Christ. Billy Graham prayed for all those who had come to the front; a man came over to write down details of each person's address so Bible studies could be sent out which I received, and I enjoyed the Bible lessons which I completed within the year.

At the end of grade 7, we sold the house and moved to a rental property nearby, an old wooden Queenslander house. I graduated to high school, catching the early morning bus to attend. There were 1,000 students who attended this school, and I felt completely detached. None of my friends were in my class or indeed even at the school. However, I decided to participate in activities, joining the choir and receiving dancing lessons, which greatly embarrassed me. The problem was that my hands perspired profusely in the heat; therefore, holding my partner's hands, I would be dripping wet, so I wore white gloves. We also did cooking at school and had to take the exact ingredients in little containers, and invariably, I would leave some ingredient behind and so my cooking would turn out disastrously!

One morning, Dad had received his newspaper as usual. The headlines showed the news for the day – there was to be an eclipse of the sun. At the end of the day and while waiting for the bus, I defiantly gazed into the cloudy skies thinking *could the sun do damage to my eyes through the clouds?*

A short time later, I was sitting at the back of the class and noticed that the teacher's handwriting on the blackboard seemed small. I walked straight up to Miss and said so. That evening I mentioned it to Dad who, picking up the newspaper, said, 'Sharon, walk over to the other side of the lounge room and read this heading.' I could not. 'We will need to book an appointment for an eye test,' which was promptly arranged. I did not pass the eye test and glasses were to be made for my near-sightedness: *horror of horrors, four eyes*, I thought. Those glasses were the ugliest things I had ever seen in my life, and I would not wear them even if my life depended on them.

My escape was to wander out in the bush to explore. I would fantasise that I was this great explorer and was opening up new lands as I tramped through huge concrete pipes. I was unaware at the time that one of my Australian ancestors was, indeed, a famous explorer and surveyed a route just above Sydney at Hawkesbury River. The gum trees smelled divine, the cicadas hummed, and the kookaburras laughed. I loved the natural world God had created and felt nearer to Him whilst in the midst of nature than anywhere else.

'Merry Christmas, girls,' Dad called out just before he entered the lounge where Rose and I were gazing in wonder at all the Christmas presents under the huge pine tree Dad and Mother bought a few days earlier. We had a wonderful time decorating the tree with all the tinsel, bells, and balls. 'This will be a wonderful Christmas, my beautiful girls. Come on outside, I have a surprise for you.'

We scrambled after Dad into his shed. 'New bikes! Oh, Dad, this is really wonderful, thank you.' We yelled as we raced over to our new bikes.

Rose's was red and mine was yellow; both had our names on the sloping pole from the handlebars to the support frame of the back wheel.

'Come outside and show me how you can ride,' Dad hollered. Rose followed but was a bit wobbly; she hadn't had the chance to ride as often as I had. We rode around the yard until we felt confident again. Then Dad watched as we rode down the street.

CHAPTER 2

You must immediately enter through the narrow gate: because wide is the gate and broad is the way leading into destruction and many are those who enter through it. (Matt. 7: 13)

We moved again into a brand new home which my parents had designed and built on a double block not far from the sea, mud, and mangroves on the outskirts of Brisbane in a new estate. It was a brand new year and a brand new decade from the sixties to the seventies and the hippy culture continued. Pop and rock music dominated the air waves, and the youth were experimenting with marijuana and psychedelic drugs like LSD. I was one of the 'baby boomers' (born between 1946 and 1964).

Rose and I enjoyed riding our bikes to the shops on the weekends with our pocket money where we would buy cakes and lollies. What a treat that was! During our formative years, we saw each other like rivals at times and had our usual fights – always over the dishes!

'It's your turn to dry. I dried the dishes yesterday. I'm not going to dry today!' I yelled at Rose. With her hands on her hips, just like Mother, she stared at me. 'I did and I'm going to wash up.' 'Well, you had better hurry because I have finished eating and you still have your potatoes, so there!' I scrambled off my chair and walked quickly to the sink. Rose followed swallowing her last mouthful of food. 'No, you don't. I'm going to wash.'

This was our routine most nights until Dad got so fed up with the fighting. He drew a weekly chart where we had a week of washing and then a week of drying; we still fought!

The new school was a lot smaller than the previous one, and on the first day of school, I met Anne, who became my new best friend. Anne had emigrated from England with her family. We were in the same classes which included business studies, shorthand, typing, French, etc. The next two years were great, carefree years. I did well in those subjects which drew to my future career which I had envisioned as a secretary.

After leaving high school, Dad wanted me to go to Business College. Although I was content with my achievement in high school, to please him, I enrolled. My typing speed increased through the college, but it held little challenge for me, and there was the whole world out there to explore – I had moved from the bush outside my backyard to the great beyond!

'Sharon, I'm going to find a job. I'm sick of class, want to come?' Sally, my classmate asked.

'Why not! We're only typing again today.' I was feeling quite ecstatic imagining having a job and becoming independent. We applied at all the places advertised in the paper for secretaries.

A few days later, I received a letter informing me I had been accepted at a government office as a stenographer (shorthand/typing).

'It must have been your natural talent and good looks,' my friend said when I told her. I found out that I had been accepted for all five jobs gone for; I was surprised not having completed Business College. In 1972, my wage was $29 a week. There were three other women in the office, and we would almost fight over the work that came in.

I joined the local church youth group where we met up on Friday nights, and I made many new friends and the boys were suddenly interested in me. This was a totally new experience. One night, after youth had finished, as we all left the hall, this young guy called Howard wandered over and introduced himself to me recognising me as his neighbour. He had an English accent. I had heard that his mum had died from cervical cancer.

'Hey, Sharon, did you want me to drop you back home tonight?'

'That would be great, thanks. I wasn't sure how I was getting home tonight and it is a long walk,' I replied. Before I knew it, we were going out, but it was short-lived. I broke it off because he was too moody and controlling for my liking, but the last thing he said to me was that he '*would wait until next time for us to get back together.*'

'Howard and I have broken up,' I said to Dad as I walked into the lounge seeing him reading the paper.

'I didn't believe that he was right for you anyway,' he replied, shaking the paper to get a better hold of it as it was slowly folding over.

Shortly after, at sixteen, I was going steady with Ian who was eighteen. He also worked in a government office, and we would talk to each other at length on the work phone. He could communicate well, a real talker, and seemed much older than his years. He was very confident in himself, which I think is what drew me to him; plus he owned a Honda motorbike. We went together for eight months. He was my first love, but the timing was all wrong, and I had my whole life ahead of me. We broke up when I travelled to New Zealand on a working holiday.

Stepping out of the airplane, I took a deep breath, wondering what I had let myself in for whilst surveying the airport I had left so many years previously as a child. It was like going back in time, only this time it was very different. Sitting in the taxi, I anticipated meeting my mother whom I had not seen for some years. It was a bold step I had taken, present meeting past, as I surveyed the unfamiliar roads of Auckland from the window. I was travelling all the way into the heart of the city where my mother worked at a hotel as a housemaid. 'Thank you,' I whispered to the taxi driver as I paid him for the fare.

The first two weeks of living in Auckland, New Zealand, I was surprised at how homesick I felt. I wondered what on earth I'd been thinking coming over. The hotel where my mother worked was willing to employ me as a waitress in their restaurant. The hotel provided rooms for their workers. Mum would call in from time to time to see how I was doing and fuss over me talking ten to the dozen as if to make up for all the years we had been apart. It would seem as though my head would spin from the endless chatter. Travelling to and from work by bus the previous year in Brisbane, I had picked up the bad habit of smoking a couple of cigarettes and now found I was hooked into smoking a pack a day resulting from the need to smoke, to get the nicotine into my lungs; it also comforted my sense of loneliness and insecurity. I was suddenly thrust into an adult world and I had to grow up fast. Everyone thought I was older than I was. 'Where are we going to tonight?' I asked one of the girls from work.

'Who cares? I'll pick you up about seven, OK?'

I nodded and went into my room to change. I had about an hour or so to get ready. I usually had something in the fridge for tea, but that night, I only had stale bread and a few slices of cheese, which I toasted with the cheese. I put on a pair of jeans and a snazzy top I bought recently and then went downstairs to wait for my lift.

We went to a hotel in town and met up with others from work; there were a few boys I hadn't met before and got talking to one of them. 'Dance?' he said as he held out his hand for me.

'Love to.' I took his hand, and we went on the dance floor. I was warming to dancing and the music was great: all the modern music, easy to get lost in. 'Let's get a drink.' By this time, I was thirsty too, so I agreed.

I woke up groggy, looking around trying to work out where I was. I was in my bed. 'Oh no!' The clock beside my bed showed 2.30 p.m. – I was horrified – I'd missed work. Surely this could not be right, but it was, I could hardly believe it. I now dreaded the thought of going to work.

The next day when I arrived at work, I was sent to the boss's office. 'Why didn't you call in sick yesterday? We were short as it was!' She looked sternly at me. (If looks could kill, I was dead.)

'I didn't wake up till after 2.30 p.m. I'd been out the night before and someone must have spiked my drink because I don't remember anything, including how I got home.'

'Yes, likely story, heard that many times, how much did you drink? Too much no doubt. Well, don't let it happen again.'

'Can you clear the dishes on table five?' my boss asked me a few nights later. We hadn't seen eye to eye for a few weeks because of an incident involving a few other staff members I had innocently got involved in, not to mention my recent oversleeping episode.

I went to the table and cleared the dishes; as I was taking them to the kitchen, they slipped out of my hand and crashed onto the floor, not one survived. I lost my job that night. Relief flooded over me; I was happier than I had been for awhile. I had been there for two months, but it felt like two years!

It was time to move on. Mum was sad to see me go; however, she recognised my restless urge to explore. I was generally forgetful, and she gave me the big drill on remembering where I had put my belongings and to keep an eye on them. There was fear and concern for me in her eyes as I left Auckland and the security of her presence. I had now saved up enough money to go travelling, so caught a bus to a small town north of Auckland where I visited with my stepmother's family who lived on a farm. From there, it was to the Bay of Islands where I stayed a couple of days. I missed the bus, so hitched a ride back which was fairly safe to do in those days. I then travelled south of Auckland, the place of volcanoes, to a town called Rotorua by bus, the place of pungent hot-boiling mud and steam, and stayed at the Backpackers and met many young people from various parts of the world. Napier, the art deco city, was my next stop where I stayed with Mother's aunt, then on to windy Wellington where I stayed with another relative of hers. I really caught the travelling bug fast and was having a ball. I was confident in myself and continued to enjoy the new sights and meeting new people in this picturesque country. Money was running out but that didn't perturb me.

I caught the ferry over to the South Island of New Zealand and made my way down to pretty Christchurch on the flat Canterbury Plains, when, by this stage, I was in need of work.

While looking for a job there, I found a community notice board outside a grocery store where an advert for a boarder was posted. I applied for the room and was accepted. It was the middle of winter and freezing. My room was so cold. There was ice on the inside of my window, and the grass was frozen outside. My new house-mates were a couple of nurses who had boyfriends and mixed in a large circle of friends.

I obtained work at a petrol station nearby. I acted much older than what I was and enjoyed being treated as though I were and refused to tell anyone my true age. I would party with them and drink alcohol, especially vodka, until it made me sick.

One night, we were at a friend's home when Matthew came over; we talked for ages and found we had a lot in common, and he seemed interested in me. 'Want to go for a drive tomorrow?' he asked just before the girls and I left.

'I'd love that. Where are we going?' I was thrilled.

'Have no idea but will head out of town and see where it leads us. Pick you up about ten, OK?'

We had such a lovely sunny day. I hadn't really had a chance to look at the countryside since I arrived, so it was wonderful. Matthew and I really hit it off and started going out regularly after that.

'I'm getting married!' screamed Debbie as she raced through the lounge, showing us her beautiful engagement ring.

'Congratulations!' we cried together; Debbie and Paul had been together for over a year.

'The wedding's going to be in Invercargill. You're all invited.' She threw her arms around each of us.

Invercargill was at the bottom of the South Island. I found the accent different to other places in New Zealand, people rolled their 'r's a little like the Irish.

Matthew asked me to marry him, but I declined. No way was I ready for that, and I knew that I didn't love him. I did not know who I was – I didn't even know if I was an Aussie or a Kiwi (New Zealander)!

Not long after I moved out and boarded with a Christian family whose young son Len worked with me at the petrol station, and although not realizing it at the time, I was in great need of nurturing and understanding. I wasn't well. I had a bad dose of bronchitis and came close to a nervous breakdown at the same time due to my identity crisis. Boarding with this family gave me a new perspective on marriage as Len's parents were very close and, wonder of wonders, would shower together every night. I had not seen many marriages work well. This caring mother counselled me, encouraged me, and listened to my life story and background so that I was able to become stronger in myself and pull through. I finally realised I truly was an Aussie at heart and consequently planned my trip back home to Brisbane, Australia. God had His hand upon my life even though I had forgotten Him. I was so busy *finding myself* and having a good time, I had not factored Him in my thinking. Thanks to this Mum's heart I knew that God was still there and He still loved me. I was confused and messed up feeling lost from my parents' divorce and family break-up like there was a hole in my heart. I did not know who *I* was anymore or if *I* even mattered to anyone, but this loving Mum directed me to the truth that God cared about me and loved me because He had created me. This gave me peace so that I was able to move on.

Leaving Christchurch by bus, I now felt secure in *who* I was. I did some sightseeing via Dunedin, home of gothic buildings with the centre of the city shaped in an octagon, onto breathtaking, scenic Queenstown and up the west coast of the South Island of New Zealand via Frazier Gorge, up to

Picton and across again up to the North Island and back to Auckland saying goodbye to my mum once again, boarding the plane back to Australia with five cents left in my wallet, just enough for a phone call in those days. I felt satisfied that I had visited one of the world's most beautiful countries, largely untouched, with snow-capped mountains, crystal clear lakes, and fern-lined forests, all the world's attractions contained within two small islands. In the midst of God's incredible landscape, He had looked after me despite my confusion and crazy, reckless lifestyle.

'Dad!' I waved my hand to gain my father's attention over the crowd at the Brisbane airport. Whilst travelling around, I had been solely responsible for looking after my physical needs and I was not very good at it; hence, I gained some two stone.

My father walked over and hugged me. 'You look different, my girl, but I am so glad to have you back. How was your time in New Zealand?'

'I had a wonderful time, although it is good to be back.'

I held onto my father's arm and chattered while heading towards the luggage area. It was so good to be back with my father again.

I broke down that night trying to make the necessary readjustments to my life, not just geographically but emotionally as well. Dad and I talked things through. I had moved back home after being so independent for the last eight months. Mind you, I needed this sense of security. Mother had given birth to a son six months before I left for New Zealand and was just expecting again. They had sold their beautiful house which I had loved and were renting an old Queenslander house.

'I'll teach you to drive. I don't want you to be stuck in some place without any way of getting home,' Dad said one afternoon while we were discussing jobs and transport. 'Let's go to your uncle's car yard and I'll buy a car for you.'

We found an old grey Morris Major which Dad bought for $200. It was a manual.

Next door was a large area of dirt road about to become a new housing estate and the perfect place to learn to drive. At the time, very few cars were automatic.

'Push the clutch pedal in. Now apply pressure to the accelerator while slowly releasing the clutch pedal. Not so fast! You'll stall the car! That's better. No! Not the brakes!'

Trying to teach someone how to drive using the gears, brakes, accelerator, and getting the car to move was very difficult, especially when my father did not have the patience. Despite this, I learnt well as he was a good driver, and to this day, I enjoy driving.

I went for my driver's licence and passed a few weeks later. I was almost eighteen. As it turned out, the Morris was a lemon. I remember the night I slept in it beside the road with the wheels hanging over a ditch (I couldn't blame the mechanics for that one though).

I accepted a job with a temporary employment agency and was given casual office work at a petroleum company. I was offered training as a graphic designer, but heard it would take four years of study to complete (that seemed an eternity to me), so I declined. Eighteen at last! I celebrated at a city hotel with some friends. During the previous years, there had been a legal debate on dropping the age for drinking alcohol. It was passed, and the age was dropped from twenty-one to eighteen; I was quite well-practiced by this stage. 'Sharon Clayton?' The nurse called my name at the doctor's surgery. I stood up and followed her into a consultation room. 'The doctor will be with you in a few minutes,' she said, closing the door behind her as she left.

The room was full of books and advertisements on heart problems, diabetes, and other well health issues. I had noticed over a few weeks a reoccurring pain in my side like a stitch. So here I was, waiting for the doctor. It was April 1974.

'It's a cyst on your ovary, so the best thing for you is the Pill.' The doctor wrote the prescription and handed it to me. 'It will help you with the pain. If it continues, come back, and we will try something else.'

I took the Pill as directed. No one explained to me the side effects of the Pill and what it can do to your personality. I became a dramatically changed person, uncharacteristically bitchy, so I stopped taking it.

As part of a large group of friends, I picked up a boyfriend easily. He lived in a caravan on a property and introduced me to marijuana. 'It won't hurt you, Sharon.' Ethan said while we were sitting in his caravan. 'It will make you feel relaxed and carefree.' He knew how I felt about life in general. If this made me feel free, then I was ready.

'I'll try anything once.' I took a deep drag like he did and nearly choked. It tasted different, but I soon felt great. I forgot about all my cares and totally relaxed.

'Here have another drag,' he said, handing the smoke back to me. I lost track of time. Life did feel better. My problems seemed to disappear. We were together for only a couple of months.

David, a fellow from work whom I had found attractive because of his gentle nature, asked me out at the same time I was going with Ethan; now I had two boyfriends. This created much stress arranging times to meet up, not confusing one for the other, and the situation didn't last long. I vowed to learn from that mistake.

When I went to see Ethan after making the decision to call things off, Ethan took it really badly. 'I'll shoot myself if you leave me, Sharon, don't think I won't.' Ethan pleaded with me. 'It will be your fault. I can't live without you.'

'Don't you dare put that on me! If you commit suicide, then it is your choice, but don't drag me into your decisions.' I was angry that he would use manipulation, although I didn't take it seriously, recognizing it for what it was – to keep our relationship going. Thankfully, he didn't carry it through. Deep down I knew this relationship was not a healthy one. Ethan and I had been together for only a short time, but his introduction to marijuana stayed.

My baby brother Adam was born in July. He brought much joy into the home, but I was restless again, needing to spread my wings, so shared a flat with a much older Italian lady I had met closer to the city. I lived there a short time before resorting to living back home again.

CHAPTER 3

Though your sins are as scarlet, they will be as white as snow. Though they are red like crimson, they will be as wool. (Isa. 1: 18b)

During this time, I had a second job waitressing several nights a week in a large city hotel. Sometimes on my off-nights, I would go out to the occasional nightclub and drink with workmates. I hung around with a group of old friends from high school days including my Canadian friend Diane. It was good to be free, but there was that old pull again, the need to feel loved. Before I knew it, I had bumped into Howard once more who had since joined the air force, and we started going out again. At least I knew him, and we were attracted to one another. I had poor boundaries and a low self-esteem, I did not know how to say *no* and he instinctively knew that. Reverberating in my mind were the words Howard had said to me the last time we had broken up that *he would wait until next time.*

We did it.... I thought it was safe to do so because I ignorantly believed that day 1 of my cycle began on the first day *after* my period had finished. Day 1 *begins* on the first day of your period with day 14, plus or minus a couple of days on either side, being the most fertile time in a woman's cycle (Billings method).

I left early the next morning in my recently bought second-hand pale green Vauxhall Viva. The day was really cold, and there was condensation on the front windscreen and windows. Back then, there were no demisters in cars, so I wiped off what I could and drove off. The condensation continued to creep over my windscreen, and I tried to wipe it away while I was driving. I drove up to an intersection with limited vision, going through, and crashed into a passenger door of another car. Not a good start to the day.

Within a few weeks, I broke up with Howard again. I had no real feelings for him. We were sitting in the car and he said he would wait until we were an item once more. I finally got some boundaries and clearly told him that there would be no next time!

December 1974, I had planned the holiday of a lifetime to Townsville and Cairns in North Queensland with my friend Karen and her toddler son Seth. When the day arrived, we were so excited that we had booked into the caravan park. I had a niggly feeling that my body wasn't right. The excitement of being in Townsville began to fade and worry started to take a hold of me. 'You look a bit pale, are you all right?' Karen asked, looking closely at me.

'My period's late.' I mumbled not really wanting to express my anxiety out loud.

'Do you think you're pregnant?' Karen looked concerned.

'No!' I looked up shocked. 'How could I be? I have a cyst on my ovary and we did it at the wrong time.' *After all I only slept with Howard once this month.* 'Anyhow I broke up with Howard two weeks ago.'

Still, to allay my increasing fear of being pregnant, I went to the local hospital to have the tests to find out if indeed it was true or not. They told me it would take a couple of days for the results to come through and I could ring up for them.

'I'm going to the club tonight, want to come?' I didn't want to stay in the room any longer. I had to stop my thoughts running wild. How could I be pregnant, I had a cyst, so that makes it impossible to be pregnant, surely? No one told me any different.

'No, I think after all the touring around we did today, Seth and I are pretty tired. Don't forget, we have to leave reasonably early tomorrow for the airport,' Karen reminded me, as she dried the dishes – Cairns in the morning; that was the last of my problems.

I went out partying to blot out all thoughts into oblivion. I lost count of how much alcohol I drank. I threw up in the toilets at the nightclub, decided it wasn't worth the effort, and stumbled back to the caravan park. The next day, we flew to Cairns where we checked in at the motel. Karen's sister, Marie, arrived soon after.

Not knowing the results of my test for another day and being an emotional mess, I visited another doctor on the spur of the moment; he prescribed Valium. 'The doctors prescribed Valium tablets,' I said when I arrived back in our room. Karen and Marie were having coffee, and Seth was playing with some cars on the floor.

'Why did you go to the doctor's, and why did he give you Valium?' Marie looked up concerned.

'To calm me down because I am so strung out.' I flopped on the closest bed almost in tears.

Marie, being a nurse, explained the addictive nature of Valium and all the side effects. 'Do you really want to take them?' Marie looked over at me worried. 'If it was me, I wouldn't touch them.'

'Really, are they that bad? No way.' Feeling horrified that no one in authority had explained the implications if I took the tablets; I decided to throw them in the toilet. The next day, I rang the Townsville Hospital for the results. 'This is Sharon Clayton calling for the results of the blood tests I had two days ago.' I felt very nervous speaking to the nurse on the other end of the phone.

'Sorry, dear, but we can't tell you the results over the phone,' the nurse explained.

'But I'm in Cairns! I can't come in, and I am booked to fly back to Brisbane, so I won't be able to get back to Townsville!' I was so desperate to know by this time.

'I'm not really allowed to tell you, but, in this case, I will. Congratulations, you are pregnant!' I nearly dropped the phone in shock; only other single women fall pregnant – not me. 'Thank you for your help.' I cried out as I hung up in sheer disbelief.

What could I do? Dad would reject me, and my family would have to bear the shame. My whole life was ahead of me with so much I still wanted to do, and I wasn't even nineteen yet! Thoughts jumbled and swirled around my head. Unwed mothers were looked down upon as outcasts! Karen had been engaged to Simon when she fell pregnant with their son Seth. Simon died in a car accident before they could marry and never got to see his son. I saw the stigma Karen went through while she was pregnant. I had been to church occasionally as a child and knew that sexual promiscuity was a sin. Mother had two little boys by my father: Paul two years and Adam five months old at the time. Having been brought up in a 'broken home', I did not want to afflict the same future upon my child. Motherhood was hard work, and I was just not ready to be a mother.

Here I was – pregnant. I could not believe it. I told Karen and Marie the disturbing news, and abortion seemed to be the only answer. I was driven by a warped sense of curiosity to experience all that life had to offer and abortion drew me in.

Now, driven by a sense of urgency, I cut short my holiday. Arriving back home, I took a deep breath, jumped in my car, and immediately went round to Howard's place to tell him the shocking news.

I slowly climbed out of the car, my whole being shaking. How would he take the news? I steeled myself and walked in the house. 'Howard, I've just found out that I'm pregnant,' I blurted. 'I'm seven and a half weeks,' I tearfully told him.

Howard looked startled. 'That's unbelievable! We will manage somehow.' Then he looked quizzically at me.

'No, Howard. We are not together anymore, remember?' I replied in great anguish and distress. I didn't love him in the slightest. 'I've found out where I can have an abortion. It has to be soon, so I booked there tomorrow,' I said determinedly, ending our conversation. I ran out the house before he could say anything else and drove off thinking *this was my problem* and not about the impact my decision would have upon Howard as the father.

The next day, I drove alone the considerable distance to the doctor's. I was feeling a mess. In the waiting room, I tried to still my anxious heart.

This was definitely risky, but I just had to get rid of the evidence of my immoral conduct. I *must* not think!

'Sharon Clayton?'A man called out as he walked into the waiting room. I stood up and followed him down the long passageway into a fairly large room. He pointed me to a chair next to his desk and then seated himself. 'What can I do for you?' he asked. 'Are you here because you are ill?'

'No.'

'Is it because you want to have a health check?' I shook my head, looking anywhere but at him. 'To have blood tests?'

I was too shy to say anything, so I shook my head again.

The doctor further asked, 'Were you after a script for the Pill?' Again I shook my head.

He asked finally, 'Are you here because you are pregnant?' I looked at him and whispered, 'Yes.'

After acknowledging my intent to terminate the pregnancy, the doctor then directed me to lie on the patient bed.

I did as I was instructed. Looking to my surroundings, I noticed a cold, steel steriliser with instruments in it above and to the left of me, attached to the wall. I felt as cold and as detached as those instruments. The doctor did not tell me what he was going to do or what to expect. There was no counselling. He instructed me to put my heels towards my bottom and then open my knees wide. He inserted one of the instruments deeply inside me causing discomfort as he prodded and pushed inside my body. The intense pain hit me immediately, and my stomach cramped and I bled profusely. He induced the abortion that was to come, and indeed, there was worse to come. I lay there slowly beginning to realise the consequences to my actions. I had given little thought to the ongoing ripple effect this would have.

Home again, yet all alone, because the family weren't due to return from holidays.

Guilt and pain washed over me again in waves. I reflected on how I hated myself yet again for the umpteenth time after I left the surgery. How had I gotten myself into this predicament? I was an attractive young woman to look at from the outside, but inside I was broken.

I slept fitfully that night having strong contractions in my stomach, bleeding excessively, thinking that my body had turned into an unrelenting monster. Next morning, I woke up weak and confused. I'd made it through the worst night of my existence. Was this really happening to me, or was all this a nightmare? I looked down at the blood-soaked sheets and mattress and remembered that this was real. Wearily, I gathered the sheets in my arms to soak in the laundry to try and hide the revealing evidence.

I did not feel so good, but at least the contractions had slowed down a bit. I hopped in the shower to try and clean myself. My family were returning today, and as I thought about them, I heard the car pull up in the drive. I greeted them at the door putting on a good act.

'How was your time up north with your friend, dear?' enquired Mother as she took out one of the babies from the car.

'Oh great, thanks,' I lied. 'We had a wonderful time, and we took the ferry over to Magnetic Island and hired a mini-moke to drive around in. How was your holiday?'

'We enjoyed ourselves, and Rose was a help with the boys,' she replied, preoccupied with her sons.

Dad walked inside after carrying the luggage in. He put the kettle on.

I blurted out to no one in particular, 'By the way, if I seem a little squeamish, it's because I'm suffering from gastro.'

'You must promise not to tell Mum and Dad,' I pleaded, then relayed the events of the past week or so to Rose.

'What!' Rose could hardly believe her ears. 'Oh no! You will regret having an abortion one day, you know,' she informed me foretelling my future.

'No, no, I won't!' I argued defensively. 'I don't love Howard, and anyway, you never liked him, besides we have broken up,' as if this was reason enough to justify my actions. I had a steely determination to never regret the decision I had made over ending my baby's life. I heard a gentle knock at the front door and got up to see who it was as Mother was attending to her baby son.

My friend Karen was at the doorway to check up on me to see how I was going.

'Oh, hi there,' I stammered guiltily. 'You're back already?'

'Yes,' she answered. 'Just seeing how you are feeling?'

'OK,' I said matter-of-factly, numb, when a sudden piercing pain overtook me just at that moment and I ran to the toilet hoping it was not occupied. The unwanted lifeless embryo propelled out of my body, and I looked down in horror at the jelly-like mass I saw there. I flushed it down the toilet.

CHAPTER 4

You are the temple of the living God. (2 Cor. 6: 14–16)

I WAS NINETEEN AND MOVED out of home for the third time into an old divided Queenslander house, with another woman called Cherie, very close to the city. Rose also moved into one of the spare bedrooms.

Diane came into my room looking unhappy.

'What's the matter?' I was concerned Diane may have had some bad news. 'We can't go to Canada.' She had tears running down her face. 'I so wanted to go home. It's been years since I've been back.' Her mother had been in Canada for almost six months visiting Diane's three older sisters. 'But we're already booked and leaving next week, what's happened?'

This was my dream come true crashing into miniature pieces all over the floor. Diane and I had been saving madly to fly over and surprise her mum.

'I rang Mum and told her. She vehemently told us not to come over because there is little work for either of us.'

'What will you do? Should we still go?'

'No. Mum will be really upset if we went over now after telling us not to go.'

As disappointing as it was at the time, looking back now, I realise we hadn't quite saved enough money to go anyway.

My car situation had changed. I had seen a beautiful white Toyota Corolla for sale in a car yard and had decided to trade in my present Vauxhall Viva and buy it on hire purchase. I later found out that when they were driving my old car away, the motor blew up. I'd had no idea of the poor condition my car had been in, much like my life!

Instead of going to Canada, Diane and I thought we would go to Port Macquarie in New South Wales to look for work, so we ventured out into the big wide world on our own with my new car packed to the hilt. We felt so carefree. Were we deceived in a big way!

Rose remained in the Queenslander sharing the house with Cherie for another three more months after I left, leaving soon after Cherie's boyfriend moved in.

'As much as I like it here, there's no work. Unemployment benefits don't really give you much to live on,' I said as I threw myself onto the bed in our seaside holiday accommodation. The location was beautiful – crystal clear waves crashing on the white sandy beach, the sun shining over the water, making the waves sparkle as they reach the shoreline.

'I'm sure something will come up soon. Did you apply for the secretarial job?'

'Yes, but it's already taken. No one wants to employ new people. What are we going to do?'

'Let's go to the pub for tea tonight. I'm sick of the junk we're cooking lately.' Diane hated cooking at the best of times, and I'm no better, boiling water is about our extent of cooking and even then it boils dry!

The pub was not far down the street, along the main road. When we arrived, we caught up with a few people we had become friendly with over the last few weeks.

'Hi, guys,' one of the men called out as we entered.

'Move over, Lex, let the girls sit,' Carl said as we made our way to the table. Lex smiled as he moved around the table. 'Meet Jacko and his brother Ashley. This is Sharon and Diane,' Carl said.

Jacko took my attention right off. The half-brothers were aboriginal, and their skin a deep brown, dark hair. The boys nodded in acknowledgement. 'What will you have to drink?' Ashley asked. We gave him our order.

The boys continued on with the conversation they were having before we arrived.

Over the night and the next few days, I found I was making a point to be where Jacko was. He had a gentle manner about him and never seemed to offend anyone. A group of us would get together and smoke bongs.

One night, Diane and I were getting ready to go out when I picked up a quarter of a tablet someone had given me earlier in the day.

'Have you ever tried LSD, Diane?' I asked while looking at the tablet in my hand.

'Can't say I have,' Diane replied while applying her make-up in the bathroom.

'Hmm, well, I think I might try this.' And with a glass of water, I swallowed the tablet.

I didn't feel anything for a while and felt disappointed. I went outside and then raced back into the room to look for my umbrella. It had started raining.

'What do you think you're doing, Sharon?' Diane asked as she followed me outside.

'It's raining. We'll get wet if we don't take the umbrella,' I said stating the obvious.

Diane stared in disbelief. 'Sharon, it's not raining. The sky is clear, and the moon is over the water. What's wrong with you?'

I looked up laughing. 'It's raining, Diane, and you'll get wet if you don't have an umbrella.'

I never experimented like that again because I did not like the loss of control over my life. At this stage, I was beginning to recognize some of the ramifications of my bad decisions, thank God!

After a while, we didn't really look for work – we were having too much of a good time. Jacko didn't seem that committed to me, so I got hooked on his brother Ashley. Ashley moved to Sydney, so I thought I would get a lift with a couple of people I had just met and travel to Sydney with them. I needed work desperately because the money was running out, fast.

I found a boarding house to live in and then found Ashley, but he wasn't interested in me. I was like a lovesick puppy. I had always been the one who dumps, not the other way round. I didn't think I would recover.

I got a job in a clothing shop in the heart of Sydney and lasted half a day, melancholy, pining over him. I could not get him out of my head. Then I got a job in a large hotel as a housemaid. The pressure was on – make the bed quickly and perfectly, clean the bathroom, straighten and tidy everything, and vacuum the floor. We had to churn out the completed rooms in a ridiculously short frame of time. I lasted four days. The radio would be switched on, and one mournful love song I identified with was one of the top ten. It did not help me recover from this unrequited love, but it was good to have a taste of my own medicine.

I found a job working as an usherette in Sydney's grand old palatial picture theatre. I liked it because I was able to see the latest films although I was only catching bits here and there, if you know what I mean.

Sydney was so different to Brisbane with the roads going any-old-where. It's a city renowned worldwide for its Harbour Bridge and Opera House and magnificent waterways including Botany Bay. Its history, as schoolchildren, was drummed into us, where the First Fleet of convicts in eleven ships landed. Amongst these were my two ancestors, Charles Peat, convicted of assault and highway robbery, and Hannah Mullens, falsely accused of forgery and given a lifetime sentence, with her three-year-old daughter in tow.

Looking for love again! I met another guy called Chris at the boarding house where I was staying – nothing unusual for me. He was from Tasmania and bisexual. He had broken off a relationship with his mate for me. He used to have a girlfriend before him. He was just plain mixed up and had been badly hurt before. He was also into the dope scene, and we smoked hash together.

After a couple of months, Rose and I decided it would be good to make our way home for Christmas, and it was time to say goodbye to Chris and we agreed to remain in contact. Soon tiring of life at home, needing money, I looked for temp work. 'Hi, my name is Sharon Hayes. I was with your agency and moved away, but I would like to put my name down for some work,' I spoke on the phone.

'Yes, I have your file here, Sharon. How would you like to come in tomorrow if it suits you and we will go through jobs that are available? Say 11 a.m.?' asked the receptionist.

I agreed, and the next day, I entered the building.

'Hi, my name is Sharon. I have an appointment at 11 a.m,' I said as I reached the receptionist's desk.

'Yes, please take a seat? Judy will be with you in a few minutes.'

I walked over to one of four tables, each with a few chairs scattered around them. I sat down and looked through some photocopies of jobs that were available at the time. Most of them were for corporate employment which was not my taste of work.

'Sharon?' a woman asked as she walked over to my table. I stood up. 'Yes.'

'Please follow me. I'm Judy.' I followed her into a small room where we discussed what was available.

'Springsure? Where is that?' I asked. A barmaid was needed there for a few months.

'About 800 odd kilometres from here. You'll have accommodation and all meals are provided.'

They flew me out to this hot, dry, dusty, and remote little place out in the bush. I had never done this sort of work before but quickly took to it. When you are offered work in remote places in Australia, accommodation is not always the ritz! My room was in the sleeping quarters.

A family owned the hotel, and their son would invite a group of young people over and we'd either play cards or listen to Rod Stewart's music.

'Hey, Sharon, give us a beer, will ya?' 'Come and party with us.'

'We're going swimming. Get the boss to give you the afternoon off, come on.'

'Where's that beer, and give my mate one too.'

I was very popular in town because I was the new girl around and there were many single men.

'Marry me, Sharon. We'd be great together. We'd work the property.

What do you say?'

'Sharon, I really would love to marry you.'

A couple of guys expressed an interest in marriage, but it really wasn't my scene. I was not interested. Commitment wasn't my thing.

In hindsight, I was unaware that every time I gave myself sexually to a man, soul-ties were formed – part of me now belonged in him and part of him belonged in me. These soul-ties needed to be cut off and broken. Later on down the track, a Christian woman prayed them off me as I named each man, one by one. However, loss of intimacy is one of the consequences which can affect a future marriage. I did not foresee how my husband-to-be would feel about me having slept with other men before him. God's design is for a man and a woman to come together in marriage, sexually pure, where they become one flesh under God's blessing.

I woke up one morning feeling like I had been punched, every muscle ached, and my head felt like it was going to explode. Some of the patrons had been coughing and sneezing all over the place. Now I was the recipient for hosting this nasty flu. I had to work even that day. I thought I would collapse any minute, but due to staff shortage, I couldn't afford to take the day off. Recognising a voice at the bar, I turned from the fridges, which I was stocking at the time, to see Chris from Sydney.

'Just thought I would drop in to visit you,' he said smiling.

I raced around the bar and gave him a tight hug. It was so good to see him again. I thought I would cry; tears welled in my eyes.

One of the side benefits of my job was the free beer. I hadn't been a big fan of beer in the past, but out in the bush and in the middle of summer, I gave it a go and got a taste for it. I could out-drink the fellows under the table.

'I brought something for us, didn't know if you could get any out here.' Chris proceeded to unroll the pouch and papers he had and rolled a joint. We sat in my room smoking while Chris brought me up on the news from home, which made me feel a little homesick. Then we started drinking. I lost count of how much I drank and smoked.

When I finally went to bed, I found myself slipping away. I believe I almost died due to the combination of the drinks and drugs in my system. I resisted death. My urge to live was strong, even though I was seeking life in the wrong sources.

In no time at all, the two months were up and so I returned to Brisbane, although I was delayed for a short while, due to the summer rains of the wet season flooding the river, which was the way out of town to the airport. It was wonderful to be back in Brisbane once again. I loved the slower pace of life in the country, but the city was exciting. It was especially good to see my sister Rose, slim figure and long, blonde, curly hair, warm and caring and a generous nature. Our relationship became a good deal closer, not just as sisters but as good friends.

'Hey, Rose. I heard there were some great jobs going in Shepparton, Victoria, at the fruit factory, and we should be able to make some money there. How about we give it a go?'

'Well, things aren't that good here. OK. When do you want to go?' 'As soon as we can I guess. I'll find out when the train runs and book us on.' The train trip was great. We watched the scenery pass us as we headed to Shepparton. We went straight to the fruit factory, bags in tow.

'Sorry, there's no work available. We employ the same people each year and our books are full.'

'Now what?' Rose asked as we left feeling quite dejected. 'I've no idea. What would you like to do?'

'It's getting late. We need to find somewhere to stay the night. Then we can think more rationally,' Rose stated the obvious. We booked in at the local hotel for the night. We had the train timetable and looked at the destinations.

'How about Mildura? I've heard so much about the place. Plus there is grape picking; we could pick up work there.' Rose became excited. This was the first time she had left Brisbane as an independent adult. She was beginning to expand her horizons.

The next day, we organised our tickets and climbed on board a few days later. The countryside was mixed. Shepparton was green with fruit trees on almost every paddock until the farming land takes over. The crops were in, looking beautiful and green; later the land changes to brown. Summer is not kind to the grass. We were looking with awe at the beautiful colours; green, brown, yellow, and in between. We hoped to catch a glimpse of the Murray River as we entered Mildura.

When we disembarked, we felt we walked into a wall of hot air; it was similar to walking out of a fridge into an oven! We staggered along the platform until we reached the station building and sighed with relief when we entered the air-conditioned building. We took a taxi to the farm where we had organised to pick grapes. Huge sheds covered a large allotment. We were shown our accommodation which was an old run-down shack. We met a few of the tenants who worked on the farm. They looked exhausted and didn't say much to us.

The next day, we went out prepared to work hard. The hot sun burnt the skin on our shoulders, and our backs were sore from bending over picking grapes continuously. We lasted for half a day. What were we to do now? I was still interested in travelling around Australia to see what this country, I now called home, had to offer.

'When I was travelling around New Zealand, I met people from other countries and they would ask me what Perth was like and what Adelaide was like. Why don't we continue on to Adelaide? We haven't anything to lose.'

Rose shrugged her shoulders and then nodded dismally. 'Why not, there's nothing here?' We caught the next bus to Adelaide, city of churches and heritage streetscape.

Rose and I found a boarding house, but money was running out fast. We barely had enough money left for food. 'How much money have you got, Sharon?' Rose asked while scrounging around in her purse.

'A dollar, and you?'

'About the same in change. Do we have enough to buy tea?' Rose looked sceptical.

'I think so.' We had enough to buy a hamburger to share for dinner; that was the last of our finances. We still did not know how to cook.

The next day, we went to the Salvation Army to get a box of groceries. Our introduction to cooking was an experience. How do you cook potatoes and carrots? Cutting onion in small or large pieces with your eyes full of water! Our first home-cooked meal was interesting to say the least. Just as well some frozen pies were thrown in. We bought the local paper and perused through the job section.

'The best way to do this is, whoever gets the first job helps support the other until they get a job,' Rose proposed.

'Agreed,' I said, knowing it wouldn't be long before we both had jobs. 'Here's one at a takeaway. I'll go for that,'Rose circled the advertisement. 'Not much else going on that I am able to do. I might walk around and see what is on the windows.'

Rose got the first job at a chicken takeaway store, and not long after, I got a job working at a service station as an attendant. At work, we'd smoke pot and then go out and serve the customers. Rose was never into the drinking, smoking scene, however. I was easily influenced by others and found it hard to say no, plus I enjoyed anything to do with marijuana because it made me forget about my problems and insecurities. I even felt happy, that I could *just be me,* and that was OK!

Rose and I found another boarding house and rented a room each. Many strange and wonderful characters were living there: a young lad nick-named Bucky with blond hair dyed red and a young girl called Sue whom I befriended and many others. We would congregate in each others' rooms. 'See that guy over there? I like him. What do you think?' Rose asked when we were in the large open design kitchen/lounge room.

'What the guy with an amputated leg?'

'Yes, he's so cute and funny. We talked for ages the other night. I like him.' 'Go for it, Rose. He seems OK, just be careful though.' My motherly instincts took hold.

'Don't worry, we're getting to know each other. Wants to travel around Australia, may go to Darwin next. But he has a good job here so hasn't any reason to move yet.'

I felt strangely alone now that Rose had met someone. I was ready to fall in love and consequently fell for an older man who was divorced. We drove up the Adelaide Hills and looked out over the city, but his recently broken heart was elsewhere.

Rose and I were lying on my bed one evening. Rose's boyfriend Adrian was working; we hadn't had a lot of time together recently, so it was a great time to catch up.

'How's your job going?' I asked Rose.

'Well, let's just say I am not that interested in eating chicken for the next meal. It's OK though, the staff are friendly and the bosses are good. How about you?'

'I am going to look for something else, but there's not much I can do here.' 'You're getting restless again?' Rose knew me better than I did sometimes.

'I think so. I have saved enough money to book a ticket on the Indian Pacific train to travel from Adelaide to Kalgoorlie. I made some enquiries to go just after Easter.' I sat there thinking for a few minutes working out my finances. 'I really want to see Kangaroo Island and have enough to fly over for a few days.'

'Go while you can. It isn't that far from here and you may not get the chance again. If I had the money, I would come too, but I can't afford the time off work.'

I flew to Kangaroo Island for the weekend before leaving Adelaide. The island was pristine. The people were like family. I didn't have enough money to stay an extra night, so they all chipped in for me to stay. Somebody from the lodge took me out in their car to the beach to see the seals. I loved it.

I still felt extremely vulnerable and insecure without a boyfriend, so I did the only sensible thing a young woman could do – fell in love with the Canadian pilot on the flight back who was about to return to his homeland! The very place I wanted to be! Canada and love! Was this to be? Alas, no, I never saw him again.

Secretly, I made up my mind that I would work in Kalgoorlie as a prostitute, knowing that my greatest asset was my physical beauty; I could save up a lot of money quickly and fly to Canada to fulfil my dream of seeing that great country. I gave no thought to sexually transmitted diseases, and this was an era when AIDS had been unheard of. Oh, how foolish my thinking was! I was twenty years old, insecure, believing I was 'left on the shelf'. I needed love so desperately.

Strange though, on the one hand, I had stopped sleeping around yet was contemplating prostitution as a career choice! I had forgotten about God in my despair – He hadn't forgotten about me and was to move upon my circumstances drastically.

CHAPTER 5

Your Father knows what need you have before you ask Him. (Matt. 6: 8)

It was Easter with one week to go till my train left to Western Australia. My whole life was about to take a major turn. These two guys on motorcycles rocked up at the boarding house in Adelaide. Chris, with straight dark hair, had a BMW, and the other, whom I nicknamed 'Blondie', rode a lime green Kawasaki 900 with matching green leathers. Power-packed, exciting, and even daring – he was a *spunk*, my kind of guy. They had travelled over from Phillip Island, Victoria, on their way to Perth. A mate was following a few days behind, on his Ducati, as well as Chris' girlfriend. These Aussies, like many others, were drawn from the east coast to explore the wonders of the west, including me.

My fascination only grew with Peter over the next few days.

Late one night, I mentioned to my friend Sue that I liked 'Blondie'. His obvious features were his halo of long blonde hair and his beaming smile revealing large, strong, even teeth. I was attracted to the opposite of what I saw in myself. 'Do you want me to bring him over?' she asked.

'No!' I said horrified. I would feel embarrassed if she did. She went and got him.

'Hi, my name's Peter. You're Sharon?' I nodded, unable to speak. He won my heart then and there. 'How long have you been here?' he asked breaking the silence.

'A few weeks. My sister and I came down from Brisbane.' We chattered awhile getting to know each other.

A few days later, Peter came into the lounge where I was making some lunch. 'We're going for a ride to the Adelaide Hills tomorrow, do you want to come? I've a spare helmet.'

'Yes, I'd love that.' But in the end, I couldn't go because Sue was feeling sick and needed me there to keep her company.

The boys hadn't arrived home by the time we had finished tea, and we were getting worried when they staggered through the door. Peter and Chris came off their bikes after going around a corner due to an oil slick on the road.

The bikes were free of any major damage, so the next day we all rode up to the Adelaide Hills and made it there safely this time, although I truly thought I was going to die. There were that many twists and tight turns, I had to hold on for dear life. I thought if I am going to die, I may as well enjoy it.

For the first time ever, I realised that I could marry this man called Peter. He was a rock as his name suggested. God knew my past, and He knew my brokenness, yet He still loved me and knew exactly what I needed. I had an unstable background, and Peter's background was rock solid. His parents had a stable marriage, and Peter's father had built their home before starting a family. I needed Peter's strength and stability. He was my knight in shining armour. Strange, though, he had a certain aloofness about him which intrigued me.

Once again I had to say goodbye to Rose. We both cried as I gave her my last hug before turning into Peter's arms. The hardest thing I had to do was leave Rose and Peter at the station in Adelaide. My heart nearly broke. Here was my sister whom I loved dearly; and the man I believed I would marry one day and I was leaving him, even if it was for only a week! Peter and his mates were going to ride to Kalgoorlie, over the Nullarbor. We promised to meet at the caravan park in the gold-mining town of Kalgoorlie.

I stepped on the train and walked down the passageway to my little room. Opening the door, I scanned the room quickly, a bunk bed by the window, small table, and two chairs to one side and a small bench with wardrobe on the other. Shared bathroom/toilet was down the hall.

I threw my bags in the room as I raced to the nearest window. Opening it, I called to Peter and Rose. They ran over to me, and we said our last goodbyes just as the train whistle blew. Peter promised to meet me soon; Rose and I promised to write to each other. I blew kisses at them as the train started pulling out of the station. My heart began to break once more as the people I loved were getting smaller and smaller until they were out of sight. Since I was to live on the train for a few days, I decided to investigate.

I found the dining room, next carriage down from mine, and the bar placed at the other end. People were milling around even though the bar hadn't open yet. Others were sitting at the table and bench seats built on either side of the carriage, leaving room for the passage through the middle.

The train ride was an experience. Crossing the Nullarbor, the landscape changed continually. At times, the shrubs were so low you could see for kilometres. Nothing, not a tree, bird, wildlife, only stunted bushes and then the sand showing through the shrubs. It was beautiful.

The first night, I decided to have my meal in the dining room. We could order in our rooms if we wanted, but I am not a loner, I need company. A woman was sitting by the bar with a few other guests. She looked to be in her late forties, tailored skirt and top. Her brown hair and smooth skin glowed. She seemed to have sadness around her; I couldn't put my finger on why I thought that; just that she did. She was talking to a few people standing around her who seemed enthralled by her. After I had my meal, I decided to talk to her. For reasons I didn't know at the time I knew I had to listen to what she had to say. She was sitting alone, so it was my opportunity to speak to her. 'Hi, I'm Sharon,' I said as I sat down next to her on the stool by the bar. I ordered a wine.

'Hi, I'm Charlotte.' Then she went straight on with her story. 'My husband and I had worked very hard to the point of excess to provide for our only daughter to the point we destroyed our marriage.' It was such a heartfelt story; I was in tears.

'I found it very difficult losing everything I had worked for. I loved my husband, and now not only have I lost him but also my daughter. You don't know the damage you do at the time. Looking back now I wished we had had more time with her and not give her everything but ourselves. We thought that was love, but alas, it was the worst thing we could have done. She is now a spoilt woman who only thinks of herself, so don't ever do that to your child when you have children. It isn't worth losing your marriage and child.'

'What are you doing now?' I asked absorbed in her wisdom.

'The one thing I thought I would never do. I am a prostitute in Kalgoorlie.'

'Really!' I almost dropped my glass.

'Yes. It was all I could do at the time. I had lost my marriage, child, house, and I had to get away to work through my life again. Ran out of money and the opportunity opened up,' she said staring into her glass.

'I am going to Kal. I had thought of doing the same.' I wanted to know the details of how she started.

She looked up at me. 'Don't! Unless you want to lose your freedom. You'll have someone else telling you what to do, when, and how. It isn't a pretty life. Have you thought about the men who come into the whorehouses? You can't pick and choose who you will have sex with. Groping old men who just want to paw you, maybe beat you, and you have no choice, you have to do what they want you to do. Even the younger men who look great, they can be the worst, not to mention the cycle of drug- taking to escape from the horror of what's happening at the time. It isn't a life for you. Go find a good man.' She continued, 'I am still in the trade, but I now work for an exclusive club. I have more freedom, but it still comes down to the same thing.'

'I have met someone,' I told her.

'Good, don't destroy your youth. You'll regret it for the rest of your life.'

Phew! That was a close call. Reality hit home. I was shown that life as a prostitute was not all the glamour I had believed it to be.

I had a lot to think about after we spoke. I couldn't sleep, thinking about the path I was heading towards before I met Peter. He was my biggest distraction from the path of destruction. God had crossed my path with Peter's, in the very nick of time!

When I finally arrived at Kalgoorlie, I took a taxi to the caravan park. For the few days, I was there alone. I wandered the streets and shops. It was a desolate-looking town; men everywhere and a few women. How could I have been so stupid to think of prostitution as a career? I saw some of the women who were on the streets and the old run-down little houses the men went into. I saw the men too! She was right. Would I have wanted to have sex with them? Would I have had the choice? From what Charlotte said, no.

I was doing the washing at the caravan park one day, waiting for the small load to finish when a young man walked in. 'Hi, how are you?' he greeted me.

'Great. And how are you?' I asked, taking note of his English accent. We struck up a conversation, 'I read palms. Have you ever had one done?' 'No, I'm curious though I've heard some of my friends have had it done.' 'Give me your hand. Mmm, you're going to get married, which will end up in divorce later down the track.'

'Really? How many of your predictions have come true?'

'It's not my predictions. It's written on your palm, that's your life.'

I refused to believe the word he had spoken over my life. I couldn't accept the implication of what that would mean for my future.

A few days later, I heard the bikes before I saw the riders. I raced out of the van and waved at the three amigos. I threw my arms around Peter and gave him a huge hug. I was worried that he might have changed his mind and would not want to be with me. I was so glad I had met him before I left Adelaide or my story would have been a totally different one.

I rode on the back of Peter's green machine from Kalgoorlie to Perth. It was an experience I will never forget – the wind in my face while holding onto the man I had fallen in love with. The road was long and changed from forest to farming and back again. Then we saw Perth! Descending the range, the views were spectacular from each bend in the road. The Indian Ocean was brilliant blue. It was strange to see the ocean on the wrong side it seemed to me being west; I was familiar with the east coast. Sounds strange but that's how I saw it. We rode through Perth, then onto Scarborough, which is a suburb hugging the beach front. We followed the other two until we finally arrived at a house a few blocks from the beach.

'Well, here we are,' Peter said as he alighted from the bike. I followed. The house was a typical timber home on stilts. Not quite a Queenslander, lower to the ground. We were shown our room by a friend of a friend. Peter and I shared a bedroom.

Being the only female in the group, the fellows expected me to cook, but I didn't know how. We would have the usual marijuana smoking sessions together in a big circle.

Desperate for work, Peter and I walked from Scarborough into the city enquiring about jobs everywhere. He finally got a job doing the same kind of work he did in Melbourne as a service technician in the workshop, and I got a typing job with the Titles office. Peter bought a little blue mini which suited us. It wasn't long before we wanted to be on our own, so we moved out into our own high-rise flat in Mossman Park. I felt *secure,* my life moved *forward.*

Peter *taught me how to cook.*

Our routine was to go to the local hotel on the weekend and drink tequilas. The hotel had an open-air area, while inside was a dark, smoke-filled, noisy place, reminding me of the life I had left behind. It was a popular watering hole, particularly during its two Sunday sessions.

For something different, we would buy 'hamburgers with the lot' at a nearby kiosk along the esplanade looking out over the calming waters of the blue Indian Ocean. My life had calmed down like those waters since meeting Peter. One weekend, we caught the ferry over to Rottnest Island and hired bikes so we could take our time and enjoy the island at our leisure. 'What a way to see the island! Watch out, Peter!' I screamed, just as a quokka hopped out from the undergrowth.

Peter braked, nearly falling head first over his handlebars.

I laughed; it was so good to be free and easy for a few hours. 'Isn't it cute?' I slowly moved off my bike and stood still watching the quokka, which is a little kangaroo-like marsupial. Rottnest Island is the only habitat that has quokkas. It stood still for a few minutes and then hopped into the shrubs.

'Let's go to the lighthouse just up ahead,' Peter suggested. The riding was easy as the island hasn't many hills. But the ride to the lighthouse was pushing the boundaries! The view was spectacular though. We followed the road all around the island and had time to wander round the little village before the ferry took us back to the mainland. We drank a lot of tequilas on the ferry ride back to Perth and the sea was very rough. Needless to say, I paid for it by being violently ill.

I managed to travel around Western Australia during the six months I spent there, down to Bunbury and Albany with some girls from work.

Peter and I travelled north to see the wildflowers and stayed at Kalbarri in a caravan for a week. The tranquillity was spoilt by a massive argument. 'What would it be like do you think if we met up, say five years from now, with our respective partners at this particular place?' I asked Peter while we were gazing out over the massive landscape full of colourful wildflowers.

'What do you mean?' Peter asked turning to me.

'Well, if we decide that in five year's time we come back with our respective families, do you think it would be the same as it is now?'

'Are you suggesting that I bring whoever I marry here in five year's time to meet up with you? Why would I want to do that? Are you suggesting that we won't be together?' He raised his voice in anger.

'No! This place is so lovely it would be great to come back to and show it to them.'

'Would you like to tell me who you'll be married to and what would he look like?'

'I've no idea. What would your partner be like?' I asked counteracting the question.

'How the heck should I know, obviously I have not met her yet!' 'Oh really? And when do you think you would meet her?'

Peter looked dumbfounded. 'When I meet her, I will know!' he shouted walking to the car. I'm sure if I hadn't followed, he would have left me behind. We continued the heated argument inside the caravan, both jealous of any possible fictitious partners.

Christmas was almost upon us. Peter and I decided our time in Perth was nearly up. We wanted to go back to our own families and homes.

When the day arrived for us to leave Perth, I was the first to fly out.

Peter and I stood at the departure gate at the Perth Airport.

My heart was breaking once again, yet, on the other hand, I was excited to see my family.

Peter squeezed my hand; I turned to look at him. Tears welled up in my eyes, but I wouldn't let him see me cry.

'Don't forget to call me when you get home. I want to know you arrived safely.' Turning, he looked at me.

I nodded. 'Let's take a photo. I want to have one of you to show my family, and for me.'

Peter stood by the window with the plane as a backdrop. I still have the photo today with Peter's sad face. My flight was announced.

We hugged and kissed and then I reluctantly left his safe, warm arms. Just as I reached the doors to walk out onto the tarmac, I turned back and waved. Sitting in the plane, I was racked by great sobs wondering about our uncertain future. My emotions were really going to town; negative thoughts racing through my head such as, *will he still want to be with me,* and, *am I good enough for him?*

I had operated with plan A or plan B. Plan A – If our relationship didn't flourish, my destination was Indonesia; Plan B was that our relationship grow and we would be together forever.

CHAPTER 6

The Lord hears and delivers them out of all their troubles. (Ps. 34: 18)

'I'm home!' I called out as I walked through the back door. I could hear laughing coming from the lounge room.

'Sharon's home!' My younger brother came running into the kitchen and threw himself at me. I picked him up and hugged him; I missed my family. It was good to be home. Taking my bag, I went to my room hoping to regain some composure. Peter in Perth one minute, home again with my family a few hours later.

I noticed Rose's clothes on her bed. Walking to the lounge, I watched Mother while she tried to fold washing, the boys helping, well, throwing clothes all over the floor. 'Need some help?'

Mother looked up. 'Thanks. Would you take the boys out for a few minutes while I finish this off?'

'Is Rose home too?' I needed to know first.

'Mmm, she arrived home two days ago, should be back soon.' I took the boys out back and played with them on the swings until Mother called them inside. Rose arrived home about an hour later.

'Sharon!' she screamed as soon as she saw me. We hugged and laughed. It was so good to be back with Rose, so much to catch up on. Even though I loved my Dad, Mother, and brothers, Rose was and still is very special to me. We stayed up most of the night talking and catching up on what we had done. Rose was still going out with Adrian, but their relationship was a bit rocky. She decided to come home for a break and think about their future, if they were to continue.

Peter wrote to me straight from his heart, and we remained faithful in keeping in contact. He was very dependable and responsible. We missed each other terribly – thoughts of travelling further, disappeared.

Several weeks passed. Rose and I were determined to give Shepparton another go for work. 'Do you really think there will be work there?'

'Only one way to find out, plus you wanted to go again, so why not?' I stated the obvious to Rose. I wrote to Peter and told him of our plans. He arranged to meet us. We decided to go by bus this time and arrived early in the evening. We booked into a motel. The next morning, we went to the fruit factory, but alas, once again we found no work. Peter met us that afternoon, and I was safely in his arms once more.

Because there was no work in Shepparton, Peter, Rose, and I decided to travel down to Melbourne, city of trams and well-thought out roads with majestic, mature, elm trees lining its streets.

Rose moved into a boarding house, while Peter and I decided to live together once again and moved into a basic one-bedroom flat on the first floor of a block of flats, in Prahran, a suburb not far from the city. We found work – Peter, back at Philips, and me, back at my old job as a receptionist. On the weekends, Peter and I would explore Melbourne's many beautiful parks and buildings; the Dandenongs, Peninsulas, Sanctuaries, and being near the centre of the city, it was easy to go in all four directions. One day, we drove to Como House in South Yarra, an inspiring, historical mansion. We wandered through the luxurious house full of antiques with written explanations about the rooms. The gardens were made for romantic wandering. Peter was really happy that day. I vaguely remember him making some mention of marriage, but my mind was definitely not on marriage. I wanted to be independent and free to do as I wanted. Even though we were living together, we weren't tied legally, and I was content with the arrangements.

A few days later, Peter sat me down on the couch. 'Sharon, you have one minute to decide whether you will marry me. What do you want to do?' I sat there stunned. Marriage! I was against marriage. I saw the fighting and the heartache. My father and mother divorced with many battles before they parted. I wanted to have a marriage that would last. Not be torn down after a few short years, kids torn between their parents. Do I love Peter that much to be his wife for the rest of our lives? Would it last?

I had one minute! What do I say? If yes, then what will our future hold? If I said no, that will end our relationship, not what I wanted. Peter was everything to me.

I had to decide, *Yes? No? What if? Will it work? Am I prepared to make it work? Am I prepared to leave Peter now?*

'Yes.' I realised I couldn't live without Peter.

Peter beamed; 'I wanted to show you this so much I didn't want you to take forever to make up your mind.' He showed me the beautiful engagement ring he'd bought me and then placed the ring on my finger.

My heart was filled with love for this man. I was nearly in tears. He was my rock.

When I was home at Christmas, Mother and I discussed my coming twenty-first and agreed I would fly back from wherever I was at the time. As my twenty-first was rapidly approaching, Peter and I decided it would be the right time to introduce him to the family and announce our engagement as a surprise at my twenty-first birthday celebration.

After we touched down at the Brisbane airport, we hired a taxi home. I was filled with nerves wondering how my family would accept Peter and Peter, my family. I had little to worry about. We walked through the back door where my parents were sitting with my brothers finishing off lunch.

'Hey, Mother, Dad, I want you to meet Peter.' Dad stood up from the table and met us at the doorway. They shook hands. Mother and Dad instantly took a liking to him. Later on, sitting in the back garden around a small glass outdoor table drinking cups of punch, Peter began to relax. 'There is something we'd like to tell you. We've decided to get married.'

'Why, that's wonderful.' Mother gasped. Peter and I shared our plans we had thought of. They were both thrilled. Everybody was happy for us.

I had never met Peter's immediate family, so we decided to go down to Phillip Island on the weekend. I was looking forward to seeing for myself what Peter and his mates so fondly talked about the Island.

We left reasonably early as it was about an hour and a half drive, so we could spend more time there. We drove out of Melbourne and through the marsh lands along the coast until we came to the Island. Turning off the highway onto the only road to Phillip Island was nothing much different until we drove over the hill; I was stunned by the view: beautiful clear blue bay with Phillip Island and French Island nestled into the calm waters.

Peter noticeably seemed to relax as soon as we drove over the bridge, as if he missed the Island and its culture. He's the oldest of four children, a sister and two brothers. They were brought up on a twelve-acre property which once grew chicory but due to the market demands, farming ceased, although the kiln still adorns the property.

After we drove up to the house, I watched as Peter's mother, Jean, came out to greet us. She walked over to the car and hugged Peter after he emerged. 'Mum, this is Sharon.' Peter introduced us.

'I am so happy to meet you at last,' Jean said as she walked around the car and hugged me. I was not used to the affection offered by this woman; I felt rather shy.

Jean was a small humble lady with a kind heart, and she reminded me very much of my own grandmother, again another sign of the enormous love that my heavenly Father had for me. I found her to be more outgoing than anyone else in the family. We instantly took a liking to each other. His father, James, wore tinted glasses and loved cricket and duck shooting – a real country person.

The thing that impressed me the most about Peter was the fact he wasn't citified but down-to-earth, innocent, even vulnerable (not worldly, like me). Peter mentioned how his parents were not happy about the fact we were living together. In those days, living together was only just coming into vogue, so it was with relief they learnt of our engagement. I was told they had a special surprise for me that evening; we packed blankets, coats, and torches. 'We're not going shooting, are we?' I hated seeing animals killed, and the thought of shooting was something I didn't want to be involved in.

'No,' Peter said laughing, 'you'll love it. Just need to rug up, that's all.'

At Summerlands estate, we made our way down a track, laden with blankets and coats and torches.

'Here, Sharon,' Jean said as she began to throw the rug onto the sand. 'Sit with me.' We settled down. I was still at a loss as to why we were on the beach, freezing cold, watching the waves come and go while the wind threw seawater towards us.

Suddenly I saw a movement. I watched enthralled as a penguin came out of the water cautiously, then another and another until the beach was almost filled with tiny penguins. Seagulls tried to hinder their march by chasing them; the birds ran back into the protective water and then would tentatively move forward again only to be chased back. Finally, they would group up and then dash to the shelter of the scrub.

I could hear the penguins calling their babies, and their babies cry in reply. We followed some penguins and then watched as the mothers fed their catch of food to their babies who were sitting outside the burrows.

We went down to the Island every second weekend and stayed at his parents' place. Peter would leave me with Jean and go off shooting, with his bow and arrow, killing wild rabbits and skinning them. This was a whole new world to me. Peter had grown up on the farm and was used to the harshness of life in the country. His dad, farmer to builder, came home for a cooked lunch every day.

Phillip Island was a cold place, especially during winter with the cold blustery winds blowing off the icy ocean. The locals consisted mainly of retired folk and were indeed hardy. It was a place of contrasts. Country and town with housing estates dotted here and there, filled mainly with holiday homes. The beaches truly were glorious and the smell of the scrub unique to the Island. It is a haven for mutton birds and fairy penguins.

Peter and I constantly talked about our wedding plans. We wanted to get married at a heritage-listed place in Melbourne, Victoria. Many couples were married there. The place was magnificent, reminiscent of days gone by, and originally owned by a wealthy family. It even had its own ballroom, and the gardens were glorious.

We sent a deposit for our wedding, but then Dad changed his mind. He had just been to his niece's wedding, and she had gone back to her hometown of Charleville, in Queensland, a little outback town out west, for her wedding, so that was what I must do also. I was in a dilemma but reluctantly agreed, seeing as Dad was footing the bill. Dad felt that was the right thing to do. I was sad though because nearly all of our mutual friends from Phillip Island would not be able to attend. However, it was arranged for the wedding to take place in Brisbane, 2,000 kilometres away. A lot easier for us to elope. Which leads me to…

CHAPTER 7

Therefore a man will leave his father and his mother and will cling to his wife, and they will be one flesh. (Gen. 2: 24)

...MY WEDDING DAY – 19 November 1977 – after eighteen months of living together, the big day was here.

Peter and his family flew up, and Rose and I caught the plane meeting Dad at the Brisbane airport and going back to his place. I awoke to a gentle knock on the bedroom door, sunlight streaming through the window, as Mother brought in a glass of orange juice and sat it on the drawer beside my bed. 'Good morning, Sha sha. The weather is beautiful for your special day, but they have predicted storms and hail later in the afternoon. I'll leave you to wake up. Yell out if you need me.'

I instantly became aware of the butterflies stomping in my stomach, and I realised the lifelong commitment I was about to make and wondered for the umpteenth time if our marriage would last. I knew of too many marriages that had failed and wasn't too sure. I had no peace.

I got up singing out to Rose, 'Good morning, sleepyhead. Are you getting up yet?' as our two little brothers came running into the bedroom excitedly. Rose and I ate a light breakfast as we contemplated the preparation which was ahead of us: hair, nails, make-up, flowers. Mother had done a wonderful job of organising everything ready for this day.

I felt almost sick with fear just thinking about getting married, so I went to my bedroom and pulled out a joint I had hidden in my travelling bag for just such an emergency, grabbed a lighter, and swiftly went out as far away from the house as possible where I found a log to sit on. My nerves began to settle a little as I drew long drags, and I kept telling myself that I would not end up as another divorce statistic and that my marriage would work out after all.

I put on the dress especially made for the big occasion and walked over to the full-length mirror admiring my reflection gazing back at me. I wore a long, medieval-style velveteen dress with a crown of fragrant tropical frangipani flowers upon my head. I felt special having all the attention focused upon me. As I walked out from the bedroom into the lounge to have formal photos taken, I met my father's gaze. Although Dad didn't say anything to me, I could tell from his eyes he was proud of me.

'You look beautiful, Sharon,' Rose said, as I walked over to where the photographer pointed. Rose was wearing her bridesmaid's dress, a long blue dress with little white daisies sewn around the neckline.

'Thank you. You look spectacular yourself. I am so nervous though,' and smiled while photos were being taken.

My uncle turned up to drive me to the wedding in the wedding car and I pulled him aside.

'Uncle Ray, do you think we could pull over into a hotel on the way to the wedding?' I asked in all seriousness, looking for any way to ease my clanging nerves like alcohol.

'Ha, ha, that would be a good look, Sharon. That's a funny one,' he said as he looked at me quizzically.

All too soon, it was time to go, but was I ready? Mother, frustrated with my reluctance, urged me to get a move-along out to the car with Rose. 'Come on, you don't want to keep people waiting.' We arrived at the garden wedding reception grounds early; people were still arriving.

'Should we go around the block again?' I asked Uncle Ray.

'No, it looks like your mother is waiting with Paul.' Paul was my pageboy. As I alighted from the car, Paul took off crying. Mother looked surprised and then angry. Adam ended up being pageboy instead. Rose and Julie, Peter's sister, came over followed by my father who took my arm. 'You ready to go?' he asked. All I could do was nod. Dad and I walked up the garden path behind Rose and Julie. The sun was still shining, but there were ominous black clouds in the distance.

Peter, his cousin Rodney, and best man, Will, stood just in front of the minister. When Peter turned to see us, his eyes met mine, and I could see he was taken aback with what he saw. He smiled with pleasure.

An Anglican minister married us. I was so nervous I repeated some of the words Peter was supposed to say. Halfway through the ceremony, a speedboat with a skier behind came roaring over to see what was going on; as the boat turned away from the shore, the skier flew past us through the water and waved. The roar of the boat made it hard for us to hear what the minister was saying.

Then it was time for the myriad of photos. I thought my face was going to crack from all the smiling. Mum had flown over from New Zealand for the wedding, and we had a lovely photo taken with her. Just as the photos finished, the heavens decided to let go and the rain pelted down causing the slower guests to run for cover.

We went inside to eat our prawn cocktails which had been left out on the tables for us as an entrée. We had a delicious meal, followed by dessert, and then had some more photos taken of us with the knife in the wedding cake.

My father, who was rather tiddly, pushed the taxi off as we left the reception to go to the rather ordinary motel room where we stayed for the night.

We caught a flight the next day to Tasmania, a large island south of Victoria and Australia's smallest state, honeymooning in a camper van. We stayed in Launceston at a caravan park and ate dinner at a beautiful restaurant. I woke up in the middle of the night violently ill, barely able to make it to the toilet. I was very weak the next day and felt every bump in the road. I later found out a few of us who had been at our wedding had picked up food poisoning from the prawns in our cocktails. Not a good start to our newly married life. However, Peter kept on driving, and we arrived in Hobart, capital of Tasmania, staying overnight at Australia's first casino where we had booked. We then drove down to Port Arthur, an historic place full of contrasts: tranquil, peaceful, yet with a harsh past as this was the site where the convicts had been imprisoned. I looked across the bay and noticed dolphins playfully rising out of the water: a place of bondage yet freedom.

Once again settled in our rented flat in Prahran, a routine began to immerge not much different from when we were living together; yet there was a difference; I don't know how but marriage subtly changes things. The reality of permanence settled in.

Peter enjoyed his cricket, so the following summer he joined the local cricket team playing fourths, I felt like a *grass widow* – somewhat deserted. I knew nothing of cricket and tried to express an interest in it, but it wasn't me, so on Saturdays, I did what every good woman does, washed and cleaned the place.

We planned our pays so that Peter's wage went on the living expenses and mine was put away in a savings account to build a house. Where to build was the next question. We agreed on Phillip Island as neither of us much liked city life.

'My uncle has a block which has been laying around for the last ten years with nothing on it. I'll call him with an offer to buy it,' Peter said one evening when we were looking at house plans. 'It's a great location. I'll show you when we go back next week.' We had looked around for land but hadn't found one that was suitable for us.

'Does he want to sell?' I was sceptical; people who have land usually want to keep it, even if the land prices hadn't moved much over the last ten years.

'Only way to know is to ask.'

I let Peter organise the calls, and when we drove to the island the following weekend, he showed me the property. It was in Rhyll, on the top of a gentle slope, and the view was spectacular, overlooking the island one side and the bay to the other. The next week Peter came home excited. 'He's willing to sell at the price he bought it at with the land rates added.

I accepted, and the contract will be ready for us to sign next time we go down.' I was in my element. On the island, this was a gift; God bless him! Now all we needed was the house. We spent every spare minute mulling over our design for a house.

Adding to my creativity, I did an Adult Education class in the heart of the city of Melbourne learning all about photography and darkrooms.

Desiring a darkroom in our house in a basement, we factored it into the plans, but alas, it proved too costly.

'A letter from the real estate came today informing us the rent is going up again. What are we going to do? It's the third rise since we've been here,' I asked Peter that night after we had tea.

'Another rise! How are we expected to save for a house when our money is going into rent?' Peter looked annoyed. An hour later, Peter came into the kitchen where I was doing some study. 'Charmaine, my mum's cousin, has a house in Hughesdale. I am sure I heard the other day that the last tenant moved out and she is looking for another tenant. I could call and ask. It's further out though.' If it was cheaper than what we were paying, it was worth the move, even after adding the cost of petrol.

'I'll call and ask.' Peter went to the phone. I could hear mumbling in the hall. I continued to study, but my mind was now on the move. Peter finally came back into the room. 'She's very happy for us to rent it.' Three weeks later, we moved to Hughesdale, with the help of friends. Thankfully, we didn't have a lot of furniture. While in the house, Peter built a waterbed made out of wood – he was very clever with his hands and could apply himself to anything it seemed.

In the mean time, I had gained weight again which I was not happy about, so I attended weight-watchers with a friend, successfully losing all the extra kilos. My improved cooking skills gave me the confidence to invite friends over who were from England. David had just given up smoking while I was still smoking a pack of cigarettes a day. (Peter did not smoke.) I was confined to smoking in the kitchen.

'You should give up smoking, Sharon. It's not good for your health, that's why I gave it up. My health is too important to me and my family,' David confided to me.

'I am really thrilled for you, David. Congratulations, it must have been hard, but really, health problems?' I admired him giving it up. I hadn't heard anything about smoking; all the adverts were saying that smoking helps with relaxation. I had even heard of doctors recommending smoking to people who were anxious, depressed, and more.

'For your own health, do give up.' If anything David was persistent, like all reformed smokers. I let it ride. I wasn't interested.

One week later, I was reading the newspaper, and the article referred to the ill effects of smoking, how it caused problems in pregnancy and babies having lower birth weights, etc. I was stunned. Peter and I had talked about having children one day. I was taking the Pill even though I was extremely clucky. I didn't want to jeopardize any chances I might have of having a healthy baby, so then I decided to quit smoking, cold turkey. I consistently said 'no' to all cigarettes. I went through a packet of chewing gum a day, and slowly, the battle was won. I no longer saw myself as a cigarette smoker (I even gave up the chewies). I was feeling a lot better about myself, which reflected how I lived my life.

It was around this time that I realised I had so much to be thankful for. On my quest for a meaningful and fulfilling life, I had married a man whom I loved and who was a responsible and kind person.

CHAPTER 8

And it will be that everyone who would call upon the name of the Lord will be saved. (Acts 2: 21)

A BOOKWORM AT TWENTY-THREE. I managed to fit in time at work to read, on an average, one book per week. It was costing me a fortune. I had vowed that, one day, I would read the Bible which had been sitting in the bookcase in the spare room. To me, it was like God was on the shelf. I, like most people, decided the time to turn to Him would happen on my deathbed. What if I was to die that way suddenly and I had left it too late? And yet *now* was *the time* to read it. So I read ten pages a day.

I had privately repented of any sins that came to mind and now turned away from them and made restitution where possible. As a young eighteen-year-old woman, after receiving $200 back-pay from work, I had been browsing around a department store in Brisbane. I was at a counter looking at earrings and jewellery when I put my wallet down on the counter and went around the corner to look at something else which had attracted my eye. Two elderly ladies were also browsing nearby. When I came back to where my wallet had been put down, I discovered the wallet was now missing and realised these women had stolen it. A short time later, I entered the same store and went over to where all the wallets and purses were displayed, picked up the one I liked, and shoplifted it. I had been taught that stealing was wrong, but somehow, because my wallet had been stolen from me in that store, I justified pinching another one from there to replace it. I now wrote a letter to the store apologising and sent a cheque to the value of the wallet. I was truly developing a sensitive conscience – God's Spirit was really changing me.

By October, I had read two-thirds of the Bible, when, at work one particular Friday, a couple of odd things happened. Peter phoned me, 'I'm not going late-night shopping with you.'

'But we agreed to go tonight because it was our free night.' We wanted to buy early Christmas presents so we didn't have to do it last minute.

'If you want to go, then go. I am not going.' Peter's mind was made up, and I have learnt that he won't change it once he has made a decision. I was at my desk, annoyed at Peter for cancelling our shopping while trying to concentrate on typing some minor work when I heard someone approach me. 'Sharon? Would you have time to type this up now? We need it urgently.

Our department is unable to do this today.'

In the three years I had been there, not once had I been asked to do typing for this particular section; they were not part of my allocated section. I was puzzled. 'When do you need it by?'

'We need it no later than 4 p.m. We have to send it off tonight.' 'I'll bring it over when I have finished.'

'You're a Godsend, thank you.' And he left.

There are situations in life where something happens to change your direction you can't explain to yourself or to anyone else that would make sense. This was one of those times. Peter not coming shopping, the office worker asking me to do work for them, was just so odd to me that somehow I just knew God wanted me to change track and attend church again. It was one of those spiritual things. I pulled out the Telephone Directory and looked under Seventh-Day Adventist Churches, familiar from childhood, for one close to where I lived at Hughesdale, and found one.

That night, I walked into the bedroom where Peter was getting ready for bed. 'I've decided to go to church tomorrow,' I announced.

Peter looked at me. 'I'm playing cricket tomorrow. I can't go with you.' 'I didn't ask you. I am just telling you what I am doing tomorrow.' I had given up asking Peter if he wanted to do anything other than cricket on Saturdays.

'Ok, just don't expect me to go with you.'

'No, Rose is coming. I spoke to her after I rang the church to find out times.' Rose now lived in a unit in Caulfield with her boyfriend Bob. Rose and Bob had met on a blind date that their mutual friends had arranged and hit it off instantly and it was looking serious. Bob reminded Rose of me in a lot of ways. He was one day older than me and very easy to connect to. Rose and I went along the next day. We loved it. After church, we were introduced to the pastor, his wife, and their three children. We were welcomed with open arms. 'Would you like weekly Bible studies at home, Sharon? I offer them to all our new attendants. It gives us an opportunity to get to know each other and you will learn more about the Lord.'

'Thank you, I have been reading my Bible every day, but there are things I don't understand, and it would be helpful to go through them.' We organised a time, and the pastor came around. He gave me a solid grounding in the Bible with his teaching and the studies.

My direction was about to change amazingly yet again.

Peter would watch Doctor Who on television in the lounge room whilst we studied in the kitchen. The pastor invited Peter to join us, but he resisted. I thought it would be an absolute miracle for Peter to share in my new-found faith. One day, I posted the Ten Commandments next to the doorway into the kitchen.

Peter came into the kitchen, saw the poster, and then turned to me. 'Don't go too far with this religious thing. You don't want to go too deep.' He didn't understand that, for me, it was all or nothing…Peter did not understand what was going on in my heart and the spiritual changes that were taking place.

One day, after work and before my Bible study, we made love. The pastor came over, sensing Peter's defences down, he invited Peter to join in the Bible study. Peter did. I was totally amazed and overjoyed.

Peter came to my baptism. What a miracle and answer to prayer! The year was 1980; I was excited and afraid all at the same time: afraid of all the people who had come to see me. What happened if I fell over or if I fell out of the pastor's arms? Well, I had to trust the Lord, isn't that what it means to give your life fully to Jesus? Trust in Him and He will guide you. I have learnt many such things, and He had proven Himself many times in the past few weeks.

I wasn't afraid of the actual baptism. I had learnt that to be baptised means to openly acknowledge Jesus as my Saviour and believe in the Father, Son, and Holy Spirit. The Spirit was part of me already: once you accept and believe in Jesus, you are given His Spirit, which is the Holy Spirit. He guides you in all you do, if you listen to Him, which is not always easy. We often block out His voice and do our own thing. God never forces Himself on us or makes us do something we don't want to do. We still have our own free will which we use more often than not to our detriment.

People started arriving and congratulating me. I didn't make any scene while being baptised. All went according to plan. I was overjoyed and really felt the Lord's joy over me after I emerged from the pool. It was so good to see my husband in church, and we were there together. One of the Seventh-Day beliefs is that our bodies originally were not made to eat meat, so we celebrated with a vegetarian lunch.

A couple of weeks went past, and I was in the bedroom, reading. I had tried to keep the Sabbath day perfectly but just wasn't able to, so I prayed about it. Within five minutes of that prayer, I had a revelation. I couldn't do it in my own strength and I wasn't meant to. Jesus Christ had already done it for me, and when God looks at me, He sees Christ, in spite of all my imperfections. I was trying to keep the law instead of appropriating His grace in my life. Jesus not only died on the cross, but He fulfilled all the requirements of the law completely. I can add nothing to it. It is already done. It is hard for us to receive the free gift of eternal life because we feel that somehow we have to earn it. We're deceived into believing the lie that we have to work for our salvation.

I suddenly felt a shift in the way I perceived things: before I understood spiritual concepts in my head, but now, I understood it in my heart or some like to call it their spirit. I found a new freedom that allowed me to let go of doing things in my own strength and to trust in God which once again changed my life; I was a new person. I was truly delivered from darkness and confusion.

In the worldly sense, I was very thankful that Peter and I married; I truly believe the provision of a husband was from God even before I reconnected to God. I mean, I was considering prostitution just prior to meeting Peter and now here I was married to my 'rock', and I was a born-again Christian believer committed to the 'Rock' Jesus. I was excited about the rest of my life, and I had peace.

I have come to realise that before we are saved, it is like we are in a deep pit, a type of pit that has no life in it, which we simply cannot get out of in our own strength or on our own. Jesus Christ was there with us the whole time with his arms outstretched to give us a hand up and out where we can fully understand what life is really all about. It is as though we are holding a camera which is very much out of focus and now the picture is sharp and we 'get the true image'.

I stopped trying to shove the law down Peter's neck, and he slowly warmed to Christianity and was baptised eight months later. Hallelujah.

CHAPTER 9

Every good gift and every gift is from above, being sent down by the Father of lights, with whom there is not one change. (Jas. 1: 17)

'ROSE, I'M PREGNANT!' I CRIED on the phone to my sister.

'Oh, Sharon, that is wonderful. I am so happy for you. How does Peter feel?'

'He's over the moon with excitement. We decided to try for a baby, but I didn't realise I would fall pregnant so quickly.'

Rose and I chattered on the phone about all the things young women talk about: what sex I thought the baby was, a boy or girl, names, clothing, cots, and other bits and pieces.

'Where are you going to have the baby?' Rose asked.

'Leongatha. Peter's sister Julie works as a midwife there, so I would feel confident having her around, plus we hope to move to our home on Phillip Island, so it's only about an hour's drive.'

'Wise move. Does Julie know yet?'

'No, I'm going to call her tomorrow. She's working tonight.'

The thought that kept creeping into my mind was that God would surely punish me for the abortion I had as a single woman and wondered if this baby would be all right. I was feeling guilty and yet couldn't wait to have and hold this baby. A mixture of fear and strong emotions swirled inside me.

Rose and Bob were now engaged, and their marriage was fast approaching. Again, the wedding was being held in our old stomping ground of Cleveland, this time at Ye Olde Courthouse, and I was matron of honour.

Peter and I flew to Brisbane, and before we knew it, their wedding day arrived, 20 April 1980. Rose was not much of a one to wear make-up, so I applied her make-up on the day. She looked beautiful. Her friend Jo from school days was her other bridesmaid. Paul was the pageboy. Bob's two mates couldn't make it to the wedding, so, at the last minute, Bob asked Peter to be best man. Again Mum had flown over from New Zealand to be at her youngest daughter's wedding.

I travelled down to Leongatha on my rostered day off (RDO) for my prenatal appointment. Peter and I prayed for travelling mercies.

After I left the hospital, heading back home, I was stuck behind a school bus. I could not overtake due to the many bends in the road. As I casually glanced in the rear-vision mirror, I noticed a white sedan coming up in the distance. At last, there was a break as we came to the top of a hill, and this was my chance to overtake. I had completely forgotten about the car coming up behind me. I immediately pulled out to the oncoming lane not realising that the white sedan was right beside me. I heard a loud cracking sound like a whip and, all of a sudden, the white car was propelled forwards and I was safe. The young fellows in the back of the car were mouthing off at me. There was no reasonable explanation as to what had just happened, but it was obvious to me that the Lord had protected me and my unborn child from being killed outright that day. Praise God for His angels of mercy – further evidence of God's great care for me.

When I was twenty weeks pregnant, I was waiting for the lift at work when I felt this roly-poly movement in my stomach as the baby did somersaults inside. I was so excited feeling the baby move; I stood there for a few minutes hoping it would move again.

Life continued as usual. Peter played cricket on Saturdays; I went to church; we worked during the week. The only break in the schedule was my appointment in Leongatha.

My appointment was due, so I drove to Leongatha and went into the surgery.

My doctor entered his consultation rooms. 'How are you today, Sharon?' 'I'm feeling fine. The baby is moving off and on all day and night.' 'Let's have a look at you.'

He did his usual check-up and then the blood pressure. 'I'm not really happy with your blood pressure, or the swelling in your legs. I would advise that you leave work soon and rest. You need to put your feet up to help the swelling. We'll have to keep an eye on your BP though.' I wasn't happy about leaving work that soon; we were hoping to save a bit more money towards the house.

At seven months, I had resigned from my job and was home doing the motherly things, getting the nursery ready and the house completely in order. I contracted the flu, and the baby did not kick for twenty-four hours. I was beginning to feel anxious. I was told to put my feet up for a couple of hours every afternoon, and yet a lot of the time I would run around madly looking for bargains while we were still in Melbourne for our new house which was almost built.

The day arrived when we could move into our new home. What a wonderful day that was! Our own home! I was due in four weeks, and all I wanted to do was get the nursery ready for our little baby. We had lots of help moving our furniture from Melbourne to Phillip Island by friends and Peter's family.

I was down to weekly visits at the medical centre in Leongatha. My blood pressure continued to stay high, which increased my anxiety. I had one week left until the baby was due, and I didn't want to miss my last doctor's appointment. I looked through the kitchen window contemplating whether I should make the trip. The driveway was muddy, and if I wasn't careful, I'd get bogged. Not the ideal situation, considering I wouldn't be able to do anything. I felt like a duck waddling when I walked. Peter was at his new job on the council, so I couldn't contact him.

I decided to chance it and go, so I borrowed my mother-in-law's red Toyota. Peter's parents had gone over to Tasmania with some friends for a holiday. I drove over to Leongatha on my own with my urine sample in hand. 'Sharon, you have protein in your urine and your BP is still too high. We need to induce you tomorrow. Go home and pack your bags. I want to see you tonight at the hospital.' I looked at him in shock. Tomorrow? Induce me? That means I am having my baby tomorrow? He waited until

I had settled. The announcement shattered my nerves, and then I left the surgery. Instead of going home, I went to my sister-in-law, Julie's place, who lived in Mirboo North, crying all the way up the windy road, ignoring all the wonderful scenery I normally admired.

'Sharon, what's wrong?' Julie ran out of the front door when I drove up her drive.

'They're inducing me tomorrow, and I have to go into hospital tonight,' I cried.

'Come inside, I'll make us a cuppa. It really isn't that bad.' Julie led me into her kitchen and went to work making tea and brought out home-made biscuits. She is a typical country farmer's wife. Homemade goodies galore. Being a midwife, Julie was able to relieve my anxiety, and by the time I headed back to Leongatha on the way home, I was relieved. I was excited at the thought of finally meeting my very own baby.

The membranes were ruptured at nine o'clock the next morning squirting the doctor's suit in the delivery room. I was taken back to the two-bed ward, next-door to the baby's nursery, to go through the process of labour. I had read my mother's book which explained that there was little need for pain during labour, so I fully expected all to go well. The day wore on, and I was managing to take everything in my stride going through the breathing exercises to take my mind off the contractions.

By four o'clock in the afternoon, it was becoming more intense. 'I'll give you something for the pain,' the older nurse said to me when she came in during one of the contractions.

'No, I'm OK. I don't want anything yet.' I didn't want any medication that may be detrimental to my baby.

'Everyone needs pain relief.' She persisted. 'No, I don't want any.' I was adamant.

'Well, I'm going to see to doctor and get an order for you anyway.' And she walked out of the room.

I didn't want anything and wasn't really in a position to know how to stop her.

She came back and gave me a double dose of pethidine (against my wishes), which slowed the labour down to one contraction per half hour. It took the intense pain away but had the undesired effect of slowing the contractions down.

'I need to push now!' I said through gritted teeth a while later.

'You can't push. Your cervix is not fully dilated. You'll haemorrhage if you push too soon.'

This extreme urge to push went on for four hours. The time came at long last when I was told that now I could push, but the problem was the baby's head was stuck at an unusual angle and would not come down the birth canal properly no matter how hard I pushed.

The doctor said he would go home to watch some current affairs show and if I hadn't delivered the baby by the time he came back, he would deliver by forceps. He came back. My feet were put up in stirrups, and the baby was delivered by forceps. It felt like my stomach was being sucked out...little need for pain indeed!

A boy! We named him Thomas. I held him with amazement; here at last was our son. The first thing I noticed was the two bruises on his head – one on his forehead and the other on the side of his head. The bright lights in the room caused him to blink. I checked all his fingers and toes, the things you do when you first look at your baby. I was totally exhausted, and Peter was totally elated.

Julie came running into the delivery room minutes after the birth as she had been on duty on another ward that night. 'I couldn't come any earlier, sorry. I really wanted to be here for you. Oh, isn't he beautiful! Congratulations, big brother.' She gave Peter a hug and kiss.

'I'll walk with you to your room and settle you in.' Julie was wonderful. She helped me with a few bits and pieces after I had been washed. I had a large cut which had been stitched, and now I was bruised and sore.

The next day, I was in shock over what I had just experienced and grieving over the fact that there would be no more children. No way was I going to go through with that ever again, and I *had* wanted three children! Although after the initial shock, I could see myself with two girls and a boy, so starting off with a boy was a good thing. (I had always wanted to have an older brother myself.)

They brought Thomas in to see me almost a whole day later due to the difficult birth I had just experienced. I could hardly believe that this little person was actually *my* baby. He had a very loud cry, and I just about jumped every time he cried. To me, he was the most beautiful baby I had ever seen. He was our son.

Thomas developed jaundice as a result of the pethidine, and it wasn't going away quickly. They told me he may have to go to the Children's Hospital to be put underneath the lights, and they began supplementing his feeds with S26 baby formula. He didn't need to go to the Children's Hospital as it turned out, but I remained with him at Leongatha Hospital until he had the all-clear. We came out on Day 12. By this time, I had come to totally rely upon the nurses' training and experience.

Peter came into my room as I was zipping up my bag. 'Ready?' he asked. Like most men, he hated being in hospitals, the sooner he was out, the better.

'Nearly, just want to check the cupboards to make sure I have everything.'

Peter picked Thomas up from the crib. He looked so happy holding his son.

'Ok. Ready.' We walked out to the desk, and a nurse escorted us to the car. 'Thank you so much for your help,' I said to the nurses. They were really wonderful and always happy to help.

I was well and truly ready to go home. We drove cautiously all the way continually checking our precious cargo in the back. I was exhausted and felt the overwhelming sense of responsibility of a new little life and that I was the primary carer.

I thought I would be fine as a mother because I had seen Mother look after her two little boys and felt I knew a little about babies because of this. Oh, how wrong I was! Motherhood was a daunting prospect. I was frightened. Each time I had a shower, I thought I heard Thomas crying. Every time I lay my head on the pillow at night, I was sure he must be awake or about to wake and need a feed. Because I was so tense, I couldn't even relax to drop off to sleep except fitfully here and there. My nerves were on edge. I became so emotionally overwrought that I would go to eat and find myself gagging on the food (unheard of for me).

I thought people only made excuses on having post-natal depression for their weird behaviour and depression. I knew I had post-natal depression. I didn't have the full support of a mother nearby, and my sister was working full-time. I had allowed fear to get the better of me. It seemed like I was falling into a dark tunnel which I couldn't get out of and my life would never be the same again, but, then I remembered the Lord Jesus Christ was there for me and that He loved me, so I cried to Him for help.

Thomas was six weeks old and wasn't putting on enough weight. I was feeding on demand, and he was never happy. 'Please stop crying, Thomas,' I yelled out to him from the lounge room while he was crying in the bedroom. I knew if I went in, then I could hurt him. I needed ten minutes to myself. I went outside with a basket full of wet washing, crying and praying at the same time. I heard the phone ring and raced in to grab it before it stopped.

'Hello,' I answered quickly.

'Hi, sis, how are things going?' Rose always spoke as if she was happy. 'Rose!' I burst into fresh tears.

'What's wrong, Sharon?' my sister sounded concerned.

'Oh, Rose, Thomas won't stop crying. He doesn't seem to be putting on weight, and I feel so alone.'

'Why don't you put him on the bottle and see what happens?'

'What! If I do that, then he will reject me. Everyone I spoke to said that the bottle is the worst thing to do if you want to breastfeed your child. I don't want to go that way.' I was horrified to think I didn't have enough milk.

'Sharon, just do it once. If it makes no difference, you haven't lost anything. But if it does, you will know what is wrong with him. Just try it, sis,' Rose spoke quietly.

I thought about it for a few minutes. If he is hungry, that would account for him being unsettled, and one bottle shouldn't make him reject me, should it? He was on it for a short time in hospital and hadn't rejected me then. 'Ok, I'll go and get a small tin.' We spoke for a good while after about life in general.

Thomas had fallen asleep, so when he woke up, we went to the local pharmacy, and I bought the milk and did some shopping at the local supermarket. It wasn't a big store, but it had most of the essentials.

I gave Thomas the bottle, and he slept for twelve hours. I had to check on him regularly as I began to worry something was wrong. But he was just as tired as I was, he needed the sleep, and slept twelve hours every night from then on.

My new life as a mother became normal, and I enjoyed motherhood although I was disappointed that I could not breastfeed Thomas for longer. We tried giving Thomas a dummy, but he kept spitting it out, so I no longer bothered. He loved his bottle though and absolutely thrived on it, gaining weight rapidly. He was a beautiful baby and brought Peter and me much joy. God had shown His goodness and mercy to me; I just needed to believe the Word of God. All was well.

Our young family worshipped God with a small group of fellow believers, three older couples, on Saturday afternoons at a shop in Cowes. We had Thomas dedicated to the Lord in our home with our lounge room full of friends and loved ones.

Before we knew it, Thomas celebrated his first birthday party with a few of his little friends who were around his age. He was asleep when they all turned up, and upon wakening seemed a trifle confused with all the fuss. My decision not to have children after the birth of Thomas disappeared.

I now wanted to have a baby again and was cluckier than ever. After having Thomas, I learnt how to read my menstrual cycle and found out about the Billings method. Peter and I thought that this would be a good time to try for another baby, but before we had the chance to try, I had already fallen pregnant. I thought my stomach felt a little heavier. I had no morning sickness whatsoever this time, and, at fourteen weeks, I had the first ultrasound scanning. While looking at the screen, I felt this tremendous kick. I could see my baby using my uterus like a trampoline. I could hardly believe it was possible at this early stage in my pregnancy.

We were covered with private health insurance, and my local doctor, who was also an obstetrician, was going to deliver the baby, Leboyer style, where a baby is born in a dim-lit room with minimum stress and trauma to the newborn. The pregnancy progressed well, although at one stage I needed to fill out a kick chart because the baby's kicking seemed to have slowed down.

A week before my due date, I was making the bed and tidying up in the bedroom when I felt a trickle of water running down my legs. I stood shocked. I felt no contractions and nothing seemed to be ready for this child to come yet. Racing to the phone, I called my local doctor. Jean offered to take Thomas when I called her, and then I went to the doctors.

As soon as I arrived at the surgery, I was taken into the examination room. 'Won't be long, Sharon. The Doctor knows you're here,' the receptionist said as she offered me a chair.

'Thanks.' I waited for about five minutes.

'Ok, Sharon, let's see what is happening,' the doctor said as he entered the room.

I climbed onto the examination bed. It was like climbing Mt Kosciusko! Or Everest!

He prodded and probed. Not the most comfortable examination.

'It's a hind water leak. We need to put you in hospital to reduce the risk of infection. I'll see you tonight about 6 p.m.' He noted my apprehension. 'This does happen from time to time. Your baby is doing well. It really is just a precaution.' I nodded, not trusting my voice. He escorted me to the desk and handed me to one of the receptionists and explained quietly his request.

The arrangements were made; all I had to do was go home and get my bag.

I rang Peter as soon as I walked in the door. 'Is it that serious?' Peter asked. He was still at work and wouldn't be home for hours.

'Don't think so, but he wanted me in as a precaution.'

'Ring Mum and ask if she would continue to look after Thomas. She was taking him anyway when you come into labour.' Peter's mother was delighted to have Thomas. She loved him as much as we did.

Hospitals can be so boring, especially when you are waiting for your baby to come into the world and nothing happens. I was in for a couple of days when I suddenly felt a weird feeling in my abdomen, mini-explosions going off at the top of my stomach. (It felt like the baby was playing games with his fingers and toes.)

The next day, as I had not begun contracting, the doctor decided to hook me up to a drip to bring the labour on. What should be on television that morning but a woman giving birth!

When Peter arrived, I sent him off to buy me a coffee scroll. I was ravenous and scoffed it down like it was my last meal. 'Thanks,' I said after I finished it. 'I needed that.'

This time, the labour seemed like one long contraction. I feared the worst after the long difficult labour I had gone through with Thomas, but things were progressing well this time. I had the reassurance of knowing a little of what to expect (I hate not knowing what to expect). As the doctor walked in, I asked Peter to get up on the bed behind me to give me leverage to push the baby out. I clenched the bars of the bed during the transitional stage of the labour and then my body just went numb. I felt the urge to push, but there was no more pain, and after a six-hour labour, Grant entered the world at 5.55 p.m., in time for dinner.

Our beautiful second son was placed on my stomach, and I loved him instantly. He made a tiny little cry. Peter cut the cord and carried him to a crib full of warm water to simulate the water in the womb. The lights had been dimmed so as not to be a shock for the baby's entry into his big new world, the Leboyer style. It was a very different experience to Thomas's arrival. We were in hospital for one week.

Grant had such a soft cry which only made me amused (little was I to know he would be the loudest of all our children). I managed to breastfeed Grant for nine weeks, but he was not gaining much weight, so he was put on the bottle. God loves children (whether they were bottle or breastfed) as He is the Creator of all. Grant was a different baby to Thomas in many ways. I was a different mother too – more confident and relaxed. He didn't sleep through the night until six months of age and seemed to need less sleep during the day.

Grant's first smile was at his big brother Thomas at the age of four weeks. They were twenty-one months apart. Other than normal sibling rivalry, they were the best of mates. Watching these babies, I too felt that I was young in my Christian journey with God.

Grant was dedicated to the Lord at home just as Thomas had been, with many attending.

CHAPTER 10

I have told these things to you so that you would have peace because of Me: in the world you have distress: but be of good courage, I have over- come the world. (John 16: 33)

One day, when Grant was eighteen months old, I had to do the laundry downstairs, and I left them to themselves. When I came back inside, to my horror, I discovered that Thomas and Grant had been playing with the dishwashing powder which I had left underneath the sink. Grant's lips and cheek were blistered.

I picked up the boys and raced to the car. I made it to the doctors in record time! I ran in with both boys and asked to see a doctor immediately; the staff took one look at Grant and led me into the examination room.

'What happened?' the Doctor asked as he checked Grant.

'I found the boys playing with dishwashing powder. Grant has some on his mouth. I brushed the powder off and brought them straight here.'

The doctor examined Grant's mouth and lips.

'It seems he must have spat the powder out. I can't see much damage to his throat. If he had swallowed even a teaspoon, he would have burnt his oesophagus. He needs to be hospitalised overnight for observation, just in case,' the doctor said thoughtfully after a few minutes.

A big lesson learnt, toddlers and moving babies need poisons placed on the top shelf and mothers need to be aware of what is and isn't poisonous. God's hand of protection was indeed upon every member of our family.

During this time, I was constantly nauseous and becoming increasingly unwell. I had just recovered from a bout of giardia which I believe was through the drinking water, but this was different. To top it off, my wisdom teeth had come through and they needed to be removed. One top tooth was coming through at an odd angle and gouging out the inside of my cheek, plus the two bottom teeth were impacted and needed to be cut out. I went, via ferry, to the mainland to a private hospital and had it attended to.

I began to feel my life was not my own; I should have been content, but I was in truth unsettled, and I felt I was in the wrong place, anywhere else but Phillip Island. I longed to be with my family. I had given myself to these two little people in my life, as well as to my husband, meeting everyone's needs and not taking my own needs into account. I was socially isolated, knowing only few young mothers, and my world was consumed by my growing family, and my soul (my mind, will and emotions) was out of alignment. This was manifesting itself through continual illness – giardia, my teeth, and the nausea – revealing my lack and discontent.

Each day the nausea and tiredness seemed to get worse. The boys were running around making noises, fighting, playing rough games. I realised I was not coping real well.

One morning, Grant started crying and calling out for me. I raced around the corner to see Grant lying on the ground: he tripped on a rock in the yard. Bending over to pick him up, I felt a sharp stabbing pain in my lower right side. I sat beside him on the ground. The pain settled but only a little. After a few hours of constant pain, I made an appointment to see my doctor.

Dressing the boys and settling them in their car seats, I went to the doctor's. Like all boys, they thought it was fun that Mum was not able to run after them. But I finally made them sit down quietly in the surgery.

The receptionist took the boys and me into the examination room, and we waited for a few minutes. I regretted not asking Jean to look after the boys. They found some toys in the corner and sat quietly and played. When the doctor came into the room, the boys looked around, but their interest was in the picture book they found. I explained why I had come.

'I believe it is your appendix. I wouldn't like to wait too long if I was you. It would be wise to have it removed soon,' the Doctor said after a quick examination.

'When will that be?' I asked, not sure what would happen next. 'If you could wait in reception for a few minutes, I'll organise it.'

The boys and I waited. They settled again with the toys in the corner. I read a magazine until I was called again.

'You're booked in next week at the public hospital. If you can be there by 2 p.m., the surgery will be the next morning.'

Hence I was admitted into the public hospital into a large ward for women. My room-mates were an elderly lady who had just had a hip replacement, and the other woman was dying of breast cancer. I felt isolated in my illness.

In recovery, after having my appendix removed, I felt disorientated. I thought I had more teeth removed. I asked groggily, 'Have you removed my teeth?'

'No, you have just had your appendix removed.' The nurse laughed.

'Your teeth are just fine.' Anaesthetics can do strange things to your mind.

Once back in my room, I began to feel hungry and asked for something to eat. 'You have to pass wind before you can eat,' the nurse replied.

'Why?'

'We have to make sure your bowel's OK. Anyway it shouldn't take too long.' Finally, I passed wind. I laughed and got the giggles telling everyone in the ward, 'I can eat now!' After two days, the registrar came in. 'You can go home today if you want to. Everything is going well.'

'I would prefer not to at the moment. I have two very active boys and a husband. I don't think I am quite up to going home just yet.'

The doctor laughed. 'Know what you mean, I have two boys and they can be a handful. OK, stay here for another three days. That will give you time to recover.'

'Mind if I ask something?' I said not sure if it was right just then, but I wanted to know. 'I would like to have another baby at the end of the year. Will I be strong enough by then to have one?'

'Suggested recovery for this type of operation is six weeks before you do any really heavy lifting. You should be well and truly fit and ready by then.' I accepted his decision, not thinking much about it, and three days later, I left the hospital to go home.

My cycle was all out of whack, and a month later, we conceived a little earlier than we had anticipated. I was still physically recovering from major surgery and was not in the right frame of mind at the time of conception. I had planned to try the whole diet thing to try and conceive a girl and resented the pregnancy feeling certain the baby would be another boy. I had a little nausea also.

At six weeks of pregnancy, I could feel what seemed like kicking. This went on every day, day after day. It was so odd though that I should feel these sensations so soon. Eventually I told Peter because the kicking seemed to be getting more pronounced and I was getting tired of it. He told me off saying that he wanted this baby regardless. Finally, I accepted the fact I was pregnant and regretted what had been my rejection of the new life within, and the kicking stopped until the normal time. Looking back now, I realise that this was my body's way or the baby's way of continuing the pregnancy – probably the latter.

Over the past year, we had the house on the market, creating a certain amount of stress. Many people who were buying were only interested in purchasing a holiday home. Eventually, we sold the house. I nearly jumped with joy when the papers were signed. 'Queensland, here we come,' I cried in delight. 'I can't wait.' I thought rationally after a few minutes. 'I'll miss your family though, Peter. We have become so close, and all our friends.'

Peter would be leaving behind his mother, sister, and brothers, not to mention numerous aunts and uncles and relatives who had lived on Phillip Island for generations. My heart longed to be where I had grown up during my teenage years.

I was fourteen weeks pregnant when we moved. The trucks arrived to pick up our belongings and transport them halfway across the countryside. The cost for moving the furniture was in the thousands. We arranged to ferry across to Stony Point where we would catch the train to Rose and

Bob's place, who lived in Frankston, and stay the night and then catch a taxi the next day to the airport. It was so hard to say goodbye to our family on the Island. Jean and I hugged and cried together. Peter's brothers were showing brave faces, but I knew they were going to miss Peter, and vice versa. Many tears later Peter, and I said our farewells.

After once again saying heartfelt goodbyes to Rose and Bob the next day, we caught our flight and settled the boys in their seat; Peter with Thomas, I with Grant. The flight was good; thankfully the boys slept most of the way.

The taxi stopped outside Dad's house. They had moved again into a new home overlooking the water. We took the boys out of the taxi. Peter helped remove our bags from the boot and then walked around to the back door.

'Mum, Dad, we're here,' I called out into the empty kitchen.

I heard movement and then Mother appeared. 'Sharon, Peter, we didn't expect you for another day. Come in. Well, who do we have here?' Mum looked at the boys. 'Let me guess. You must be Thomas, and you're Grant. Am I right?' The boys nodded.

'Would you like some lemonade? I think you would, I know my boys do. Would you like to help me?' This was the invitation they needed. The boys followed Mother to the fridge. Finding the lemonade, they took their glass to the table and tried to sit up. 'Let me take the lemonade from you. There, that's better. Now you can get up. Here a cup each.' Mum was great with the boys.

Dad walked in from the shed. I hugged him. It was good to see him again. 'I've arranged your rooms. I can look after the boys a couple of hours for you both while you look for a house. Where do you want to move to?'

Mum said.

Peter and I looked at one another. We hadn't really decided. 'Don't know yet. We will have to see what the house prices are.'

Peter found a job within a few days. We then looked for a house and a car. Peter and I managed to find a house within the first week. My folks lived near the sea at a place called Ormiston, south of Brisbane, and we chose to live further inland, where it was cheaper to buy. We lived a half-hour drive from my folks and closer to where my good friends, Malcolm and Canadian Diane, lived with their two young children.

The thing I remember clearly was, for several weeks after moving to Queensland, I had blinding headaches, whether it was stress from moving interstate or the bright glare I don't know, but I practically lived on panadol (headache tablets).

The day arrived when we moved into our new home after staying with my folks for five weeks. Although it was good to live with them, it was a relief to move into our own home.

Peter and I drove to our new brick home. We had our furniture in storage, so I was excited to see the trucks pull up, and the men started unloading our belongings. I directed the workers as to where each box and furniture piece would go. I put the two boys in one room, and another bedroom was to be for the new baby. Peter and I had the corner bedroom. The lounge was separated from the kitchen and a huge backyard for the boys to play in. When the final box was put down and the trucks left, Peter and I looked at each other. 'This is home now, finally.' Peter was as excited as I was to have our own home again.

'We need to sort a few things out before we get the boys.'

We started unpacking the kitchen; boys still need to be fed. Then their bedroom, clothes sorted in drawers and beds made up, then ours. For the lounge, we bought a new, cream-coloured, chunky lounge suite which could easily be rearranged to suit the room. At least that was a start; the rest could be done over the next few days. We found out the hard way our new home had no air flow through it and that it was a very hot house.

Then as a 'welcome' present into our new home, we all came down with the *flu.* I needed antibiotics even though I was pregnant. How life brings on challenges for us! In the first year, the boys were constantly unwell as we acclimatised to the warmer weather. Thomas already had a weakness in his chest and frequently needed antibiotics for bronchitis just as his father and grandfather had done before him. Grant tended to get tonsillitis frequently just as I had done as a toddler requiring antibiotics. It was not an easy time.

As my pregnancy progressed, I gained a substantial amount of weight. I found myself becoming more maternal, and I deeply regretted the way in which I had rejected the pregnancy earlier on. I loved this child dearly even before birth.

History repeated itself. Ten days before the due date, once again I was making the bed and tidying up in the bedroom when I felt a trickle of water running down my legs – hind water leak. This time I was not shocked, but I did feel anxious. I was booked into the new hospital in town.

'Peter,' I called out to my husband who was playing with the boys outside. Peter raced in to see what was wrong. 'I need to go to the hospital.'

'Now? Have you had any contractions?'

'No, but I think my hind water has leaked. Last time I had to stay in hospital.' I reminded him. We dropped our two young sons at my friend's place. When we arrived at the hospital, we were directed into a waiting area until the doctor arrived. He escorted us into a room where I was examined.

'I won't be long. I need to see what we can do now,' the doctor said. Peter and I waited for a few minutes and then I felt a contraction. Now, I felt justified being there. Peter looked worried while I held onto his hand. 'I think I just had a contraction,' I said just after the pain subsided. Peter didn't wait. He stood up and left the room.

A few minutes later, he and the doctor walked back in. 'This changes everything. The nurse will take you to your room.' I wasn't sure whether

I was in labour or not, but as it turned out, I actually was. I was totally amazed that I had gone into labour all by myself naturally.

The hospital was near the university, and the doctor asked if some students could observe the baby's delivery. By this stage, I couldn't have cared less, so I said yes. There must have been over twenty people in the room! I wanted the midwife to cut me so I could deliver the baby. The midwife refused, (that had now gone out of fashion) so consequently I tore. The baby's heartbeat had slowed right down – they realised their mistake and cut me, after urgently injecting the area. I screamed! There had been no time for the injection to work. The students witnessed the arrival of our third son Jethro born on 8 August 1985, weighing 8 pounds 8 ounces after a four and a half-hour labour (he was in a hurry). He was born with his little arm up around his head with the cord wrapped around both arm and neck. When they put him on my stomach, the first thought I had was *I would never have the opportunity to put my baby in little dresses.* I should have been more thankful, but we had only planned on having three children. He was my last chance at trying for a daughter. He was a long baby and fine-looking. My beautiful third-born son was such a gift to Peter and myself. There was a three-year age gap between Grant and Jethro.

My neighbour Kate from across the road looked after the boys while I was in hospital. She had four young sons herself and two teenage step-daughters. We had clicked instantly, and she was a great help to me, physically and emotionally, in my time of need.

Again, I went through a short time of post-natal depression. I was run-down physically and large chunks of hair came out in my hands every time I shampooed. I had little emotional support from my parents, and Rose lived too far away in Victoria; Peter had to work. I wondered why I had brought another child into the world when there were so many already living here. Negative thoughts ran through my mind constantly.

Jethro was put on the bottle three weeks of age.

Having three little boys under five was a huge struggle so much so that I told Peter to go have a vasectomy. I knew it wasn't right, but I was beyond caring. He went and dutifully had the job done and was told it would take a couple of months for the all-clear and to be careful in the meantime.

One day, I was having a bath. Grant, three, came in. 'You have a baby in there,' he said patting my stomach – out of the mouths of babes. I was fighting a gastric bug at the time and had taken strong medicine to treat it. I couldn't shake the haunting idea that *'I had a baby in there'*. I was mortified; I suddenly knew I had fallen pregnant again. Peter had the vasectomy so we wouldn't have any more children and here I was – pregnant. The baby was only two months old. After a few days, I began to get used to the idea. Then the unthinkable happened. I miscarried. Jethro and the baby would have been only eleven months apart.

A feeling of grief threatened to overwhelm me, but Mother consoled me, having been through a similar experience. I also privately grieved over the finality of the fact that there would be no more babies and questioned myself, did the Lord want to give me more babies?

We attended a nearby Seventh-Day Adventist church dutifully, and Jethro was dedicated to the Lord, but my relationship with God was not particularly strong at that time. I felt overburdened with motherhood, and I had gone back to the belief that religion was by rules and not a personal relationship.

One day, a lady came up to me at the greengrocers admiring Jethro. 'You have a beautiful baby. What's his name?'

'Jethro. He is our third child.' I was pleased to have others admire my son. 'A word of caution: be careful about leaving him in the shopping trolley in case someone tries to steal him.' Then she turned and walked down a grocery aisle. I stood there with my mouth open. Stealing babies? The thought had never occurred to me of that possibility.

Health-wise, I seemed to be fighting one virus after another which Thomas brought home from pre-school. Because I was feeling unwell, I became increasingly bossy, and Peter tried his best to please me. At one stage, during spring, which is warm in Brisbane, we all came down with another strain of flu, 'this time a stomach flu'.

When you have children, life seems to revolve around the doctor's surgery. One day, I took one son to the local doctor, the next day another son, then on the third day, it was the baby's turn until finally it was my turn. I sat in the doctor's office crying because we never seemed to be well. I was completely overwhelmed at the huge task of not only caring for two active young sons and a sickly baby but also meeting the needs of my husband and myself. Of course my own needs came last every time. The doctor said something which became self-fulfilling, 'Don't worry, more than likely, you won't need to come in for another six months.'

Jethro was around five or six months old at the time, and six months later, we were back at the doctor's with him clearly unwell. I learnt the hard way that it really is true what others had previously told me, *'It does not matter what sex the baby is, as long as the baby is healthy'*. I realised towards the end of Jethros first year that I had a sickly baby on my hands. Jethro was miserable – looking malnourished with long skinny legs, bloated belly and sunken eyes. He had diarrhoea on a weekly basis. I had to put him on soy milk in the early months and discovered he was allergic to bananas. Bananas went right through him. Jethro's ears were infected, and he was prescribed antibiotics. 'I am still concerned that Jethro has to go back onto antibiotics for his ears again. This is about the sixth lot. Isn't there anything you can do?' I asked the doctor again, frustratingly. He would come off the antibiotics a couple of days and need to go back on them again – clearly, there was something wrong.

'I can test his hearing.' The doctor used a little meter for testing his ears. 'Mmm, he seems to have trouble hearing. I suggest you take him to an ear, nose, and throat specialist. Here, this is the phone number.' He handed me a card with the ENT specialist's name, number, and address. I rang as soon as I arrived home.

'The next available appointment will be two months from now. I will book you in. If there is any cancellation, we will call you,' the receptionist said. I hung up disappointed. Jethro was steadily deteriorating, and my maternal instincts told me that, even though we were booked in to see this particular much-in-demand specialist, we could lose him.

'I don't know what to do. I am so worried about him. It will be months before he can see this specialist,' I told Mother one day when we called around to visit.

'Remember Adam had all those ear problems when he was younger and saw a specialist? I still have his card. Ring him now and see if you can make an appointment. He is semi-retired and it might be easier to get in to see him.'

I went over to the phone, and within five minutes, I had an appointment for the end of the week. Peter and I took our little son Jethro to see the specialist.

'Well now. I do believe he will need grommets in his ears. I can organise the operation, say in two days' time, if that is suitable for you.' I couldn't believe our good fortune. 'Yes, that will be wonderful. Thank you'. I was so relieved.

The operation was to cost us $1,000, which was a lot of money for us at the time, but our son's health was our top priority.

We arrived at the hospital very early the day of Jethro's operation. 'Jethro,' I said to the receptionist.

My heart was wrung out waiting for my baby's turn to be whisked away to theatre. I was feeling so distraught that I found myself running to the toilet. The nurses took him from me at the lifts, and they left with him crying and me feeling helpless. Peter was there with me, yet we felt apart in our own private thoughts and fears.

Finally, Jethro was back in my arms all groggy. We waited for the specialist to visit us before we left. 'I've never seen a child with so much goo in his ears. His adenoids had been completely infected, and, coupled with the infection in both ears, was poisoning his entire system,' the specialist said. I was so relieved that the operation was over. God hadn't left me – I needed to trust Him more and to remember His unfailing love for me and my family.

We took our little fifteen-month-old son home, and he rapidly recovered. The next day, he was standing at the sliding door in the dining room looking outside when I came around the corner, and he almost jumped a few feet in the air because he heard my footsteps. He used to lip-read whenever I spoke to him before the operation, which he continued to do, but, because he was able to hear, he learnt to speak earlier than most children his age. Jethro, my amazingly brave, meant-to-be, great destiny baby boy; God has a great destiny for you. Your name means 'God's peace' – Let Jesus rest on you, darling boy.

Nine months earlier, after much deliberation, we decided to put our house on the market. In Queensland, the house rates needed to be paid twice per year, not once, as in Victoria. I personally disliked the process of house-selling, inspections etc., especially with young children.

Nine months later, a group of people who had been through our house put an offer on it which we accepted. The offer was lower than what we were asking for, but we were keen to sell. Then the offer fell through. It was nearly time for Peter's annual holidays and money was very tight. I was looking around for work, even waitressing if necessary, because the rates were due. We paid the rates with Peter's holiday pay which left us with next-to-nothing to live off and were desperate to sell the house.

'I really don't want to go back to Phillip Island, Peter. I would like to stay here or even up north further.' We had talked about where we would move to once we sold, but I had purposely avoided even discussing Phillip Island as an option.

'I know, but it seems the only place to go back to. I am not prepared to go further north and so far the job prospects are not that good here at the moment. At least I can get a job back on the Island.'

'Let's leave it to God. If we are to move back to the Island, then the house must be sold tomorrow. If we are to go north, then it won't.'

'You know what will happen if it is sold tomorrow?' Peter seemed happy with the idea.

'Yes,' I mumbled, secretly hoping it wouldn't sell. It sold at lunchtime the very next day.

And so, after two years of living in Brisbane, we returned to Phillip Island with moving van once again in tow. We decided if we ever decided to move interstate again, we would sell everything and purchase second- hand furniture from garage sales in the place we were going to.

It was now very obvious where God wanted us, so I was happy to be back on Phillip Island. It had been a hard two years. Was it right for us to sell our original house on Phillip Island which Peter and I had designed and which Peter's father and brother had built to move our growing family up to Queensland, to another state?

CHAPTER 11

The man is blessed who trusts in the LORD
and whose hope is the LORD. (Jer. 17: 7)

Our life settled back on Phillip Island. There had been cosmetic changes and new housing estates being built, but on the whole, the Island was still the same. We stayed with Jean until we could find a house to rent. 'Will has offered me a job,' Peter said as he came in after meeting up with his brother Will, five years younger. Will and his wife Anita ran a TV & Electrical shop in the main street of Cowes.

'What did you say?'

Peter was certainly gifted with anything electronic. He could repair television sets, VCRs, small electrical appliances, in fact practically anything, as well as installing aerials on peoples' rooftops to receive transmission, etc. 'Actually they asked if we would like to go into partnership with them. You and Anita would be silent partners.'

'Can we afford that?' I was surprised by the offer. We had already paid for the moving and our previous home mortgage. It didn't give us enough to buy a house though.

'We will need to use what money we have left to buy in,' Peter explained. 'Will said we would be able to buy our own home outright from the profits of the business.'

'Can we make that much money?' I was sceptical.

'Anita and Will seemed to be doing well. The books look good. I have always wanted to own a business as you know. This is our chance.'

'If you think it would work, then go ahead.' I gave him my blessing. So we bought into the partnership which also brought with it a lot of business pressure, but things were rolling along. We found a small grey brick house which we rented directly behind the local primary school in Cowes. There was no bath, so Jethro had to adapt to having a shower like his two older brothers.

Peter volunteered for the country town's State Emergency Service (SES). He was called out all hours of the day or night. If he wasn't being called out, he would spend hours and hours down at the SES building with the other volunteers. I believe it was a genuinely wonderful thing for him to do, but I wondered if he had become a volunteer out of a need to boost his own sense of self-worth. It took a toll on our marriage and the family.

Grant had begun kindergarten, and a meeting was organised which I attended. I was elected as president of the kindergarten for the year and was told there would not be much to do. I used to enjoy attending toastmistress meetings when Grant was a baby, so in one sense, I was familiar with the whole idea of meetings. Being on the committee ensured I would quickly get to know some of the other mums in the area.

The kindergarten teacher who was well-liked had been there for a very long time and was retiring halfway through the year, so this would be an up-and-coming challenge for the new committee.

Again, I found myself in a role that stretched and challenged me to the limits. I seemed to adapt better that way and the only way I knew how to live my life. Thomas, my oldest, was now in grade 1.

Over the last few years, I added extra kilos. After recovering from my appendix operation with my appetite restored, I had promptly gained 3 kilos and then subsequently piled on the weight throughout my pregnancy with Jethro. After he was born, I was left with an excess of two stone (12 kg). This time, however, I just could not shake the excess kilos, so I joined Jenny Craig to lose the weight and travelled an hour each way to visit them and be weighed and collect my food for the following week. I lost weight rapidly but was ravenous most of the time. I managed to lose all the excess weight with Jenny Craig so that when it came time for the huge dinner party organised by the kindergarten committee to celebrate the kindergarten teacher's years of service, I was looking and feeling good about myself. I had to do quite a bit of talking on the stage, so my appearance was important to me for the occasion. The night came, we had a wonderful night and all went as planned.

It was during the middle of winter and very cold; wind chill can drop to – 13°C at that time of year. The thought passed through my mind, Do I want to feel hungry all the time just to look good? I resoundingly thought, no! So the weight gradually slipped back on. I thought I would be able to control it, but, alas, no. Eventually I climbed up to 80 kilos (or 175 pounds) where I have remained thereabouts ever since although does not dictate who I am.

My sister and her husband Bob had their first child, a son Jed ten months after our second son Grant was born. Three more sons came in rapid succession after Jed, and I knew that they were going to try for a girl. I told Rose I would be praying for a daughter for them. Rose asked if I would be with her when it was time for the baby to be born. I was present in the delivery room at the Frankston hospital when my niece Lanesha was born after I huffed and puffed through all the breathing exercises for Rose. We were all elated. After seven sons between us, finally a daughter in answer to prayer, all praise to God.

However, a few days later, on a Saturday morning, while sitting up in bed reading my Bible, I felt sorry for myself (in fact, I was crying). As much as I was very happy for my sister and her husband, I felt incredibly sad that I did not have a daughter of my own to love. There was no thought of it even being a possibility for me. Apart from the obvious fact that Peter had a vasectomy and we could no longer have children, I actually believed Peter and I could only have boys. Yet I longed for and needed a daughter. My relationship with my maternal mother had not been a healthy one. She would come and visit my sister and me every couple of years for five days at a time at each other's houses. We would just get to know her and then she'd go again. I would be an emotional wreck every time, picking up the pieces afterwards.

Still crying on my bed, I suddenly heard an audible Voice in my left ear say, *What are you crying for? You're going to have a daughter too.* I believed and accepted what I had just heard, never doubting for one minute that this was God, and I immediately stopped grieving, got up out of bed, and went and told my husband who also believed what I had just heard. We didn't know how it was going to happen, but we believed it would happen.

'Believe' is a very important word and is the same as faith.

Sometime later, I read an article in a women's magazine explaining a technique relating to the in-vitro fertilization (IVF) program. We explored the option further and visited a specialist who explained all about microsurgery. He asked if we were covered by private health insurance. We were not.

I was casually talking to my local friendly GP when I mentioned my desire of having a daughter and that the problem was that my husband had already had a vasectomy several years before. He told me about a couple of urologists he'd gone to med school with and gave me their names and telephone numbers. Peter and I made an appointment to see the first urologist near the centre of Melbourne. He performed vasectomies on the men in the air force. He ran through a set of questions:

'When was the vasectomy performed?' We told him the date. 'Are you in private health care?'

'No, we had to let that lapse due to our finances.' 'Is it your second marriage?'

'No.'

'Men lose 10 per cent fertility permanently for every year following a vasectomy. But I feel Peter is still a good candidate for a vasectomy reversal even though the vas deferens tubes in the testes have had a large piece cut out and burnt at both ends. I'll see what I can do.' We were elated as we left his office.

Time elapsed, and we heard no more. 'Should we contact the other specialist he suggested?' Peter asked me.

'Yes, but this will be our last try,' I replied.

We went to the Medical Centre at the end of the financial year (30 June). Peter went through the same procedure as before being asked the same questions. The specialist said that he would see what he could do.

I had my thirty-sixth birthday, and it was eight months since we had heard anything from the urology specialist. I was reading a book on co-dependency at the time (co-dependency, simply put, is when you project your own unmet needs onto others or have others project them onto you) which had the twelve steps from Alcoholics Anonymous in them and step three was to pray to your Higher Power to know His will for your life. I prayed that prayer in the morning, and at 4 p.m. that same afternoon, I received a call from the Medical Centre telling us to come in the following Friday to the Urology Outpatients and Peter would have the reversal in a month's time. I was beside myself.

We drove to the Medical Centre, and Peter, not surprisingly, developed a migraine. As we were directed to different areas of the outpatients, curiously I asked, 'How has Peter been admitted so quickly?'

The man looked a little puzzled and then said, 'The government had released extra funding.'

One month later, Peter checked into the private hospital, and the operation took two hours to perform. I felt so guilty because I had been the one demanding that he have the vasectomy in the first place. He stayed in the hospital for two nights at no cost to us at all and no pain (just a little discomfort). The original vasectomy had been a lot more painful.

Four months went by and nothing happened. I had fallen pregnant at the drop of a hat with the boys. It dawned on me that now I needed to be active in my faith, so I fasted and prayed for a happy, healthy baby daughter. Two days later, we conceived.

CHAPTER 12

The Sabbath was made because of man and not man because of the Sabbath. (Mark 2: 27)

Because my three boys were quite a handful, I joined a small group of parents at the local community centre who taught parenting skills. I met a single mother called Rosemary who was raising two sons on her own, and we became firm, lifetime friends. She was into the new age movement which believes in worshipping the universe, psychics, reiki, spiritual healing, yoga, astrology, crystals, tarot cards, etc.

One day, I lent her a book about a lady who had been into the new age movement and how God had led her out of the darkness and deception of it into the light through Christ Jesus. Rosemary read the book, and, soon after, when Peter and I were around at her place, she asked us all these questions which Peter was able to answer. She made a decision to give her life over to Christ. After becoming a Christian, she especially wanted to know about the Sabbath written in the Bible and boldly went around to every minister from the different denominations both on Phillip Island and churches in the city of Melbourne to ask them what they believed about the Sabbath.

Once a week we would meet with Rosemary and an older couple who were friends of ours, Pat and George whom we had met at the local S.D.A. church who now lived on Phillip Island. We would sing and pray together and talk about how God was moving in our lives over the week. One evening, we were talking about the information Rosemary gained from the different churches' theology.

'We have been going to a small church in Hawthorn where they hold a Celebration Service once a month and different churches and denominations meet together to simply praise and worship God. There's one next week. Would you like to come?' George asked.

'Really? That sounds wonderful.' Peter was excited. This was something we had been thinking of for a while. We all went, and it was very moving. The presence of God was felt by all as one person had a Scripture, another person a word, and yet another would speak in tongues with someone else giving an interpretation. Our spiritual walk with God began to open up as we came out from the restrictions we had been living under.

Rosemary had opened a new door for us, and we found that we were now questioning the Sabbath as we had known it following the legalistic law. I could now see that the Sabbath is not just about a day, but it's about the person of Jesus. HE is our rest. We rest in Him and we rest from all our works also. We can *never* be good enough to be saved. It's all there in the New Testament, Romans chapter 8. (However, there is a blessing for the

Sabbath day; for further reference, I would recommend reading *The Torah Blessing* by Larry Huch.)

A lot of water has passed under the bridge since those days and after looking into the Sabbath day question through the eyes of Hebrew roots (not Jewish rabbinical roots) I understand the true blessing of the Sabbath which Jesus followed. The true Sabbath day starts Friday evening until Saturday evening.

Out of the celebration service, we met some other Christians and heard about a Foundations weekend to be held in the near future at the West Baptist Church going over the very foundations of our Christian faith. Peter and I decided to go. One night, after the Foundations weekend, Peter and I were discussing what we had gained by the weekend.

'I would like to do the Discipleship Training Program that they discussed over the weekend,' Peter said.

I was shocked. Peter didn't attend courses outside of his field of work. 'How will we manage? I'm pregnant, and it is a two-day a week course, Tuesdays and Thursdays. It's a long way to drive to Hawthorn twice a week as well as work.' Hawthorn was just a few kilometres from the city. Peter would have to leave at about 5 a.m. and then be caught in the peak hour traffic, which was bumper to bumper all the way.

'I've thought about all the implications. We have to move to Hawthorn. I'll find a job on the days I have off and I'll come back and help Will from time to time when I can.'

'Well, to be honest, I think that is the direction we are to go in.' We agreed. This was a huge step, but we strongly believed we were in the very centre of His will for our lives.

The course was to begin soon after school started, so we began looking for houses to rent in the December and January. Nothing was suitable and everything was too expensive. We needed to live near the church to be a part of the Christian community, where people lived only about five minutes' walking distance from the church. We were in Hawthorn looking for a house and drove around to the street the church was in. We pulled up out the front of this old, small, dumpy house with grass growing a metre tall. Peter and I jumped out of the car.

'Hi, Peter and Sharon,' Pastor Ben Smith said as he came towards us. 'How are you going with house-hunting?'

'Not good. We are at our wits' end,' I said feeling exasperated. I had begun to give up on finding anything suitable.

Ben turned to the house we had parked our vehicle in front of. 'I could contact the owner and enquire on your behalf. He's a friend of mine.' 'Thank you,' Peter said. We talked for a few minutes more and then Ben left.

After he had gone down the path, I said, in no uncertain terms, 'No way am I going to live in that house, Peter.'

We were to stay overnight at my sister's place in Frankston. Rose and I went out that evening to catch a movie while our husbands babysat the children (a very rare treat indeed). The picture theatre was in Camberwell, a suburb not far from Hawthorn. 'We saw a house today. Rose, it is so run-down I couldn't live in it. Peter agreed to let Ben contact the owner. What am I going to do?' I shared with Rose.

'Since we are so close, let's go see it?'

We drove around and parked in the driveway with the headlights beaming straight ahead to give some light; by this time, it was midnight. We got out of the car and walked around the house. 'Sharon, this is an uncut diamond, if you cleaned up the yard and added a few plants. Put in nice curtains, it will be transformed into a treasure.' That was all I needed Rose's enthusiasm. I imagined the yard cleaned up and nice curtains for me to change my mind about living there.

The owner was contacted, and we met him the following weekend to look through the house. It looked quite decent inside with a little adjoining half-bedroom off the main bedroom and one other bedroom. There was a shower in the bathroom, no bath. Small. 'What are you paying now where you live?' the owner asked.

We told him, '$120 per week.' 'Suits me – $120 a week is fine.'

Hallelujah. God had worked another miracle for us in the elite and expensive area of Hawthorn. The two years we lived there were two of the happiest years of our lives in our little poky house with many lush, green parks around where the boys loved to go off and play.

CHAPTER 13

So then faith is from hearing, and hearing through the message from Messiah. (Rom. 10: 17)

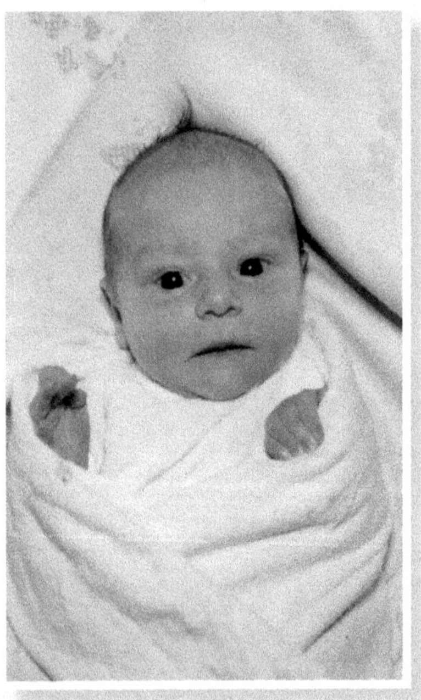

A SUDDEN CONTRACTION. 'PETER.' I shook him awake. 'We need to go to the hospital.' We had moved into the house only just over two months before.

Peter sat up and then as it sunk in, jumping out of bed. 'Now?'

I nodded as another contraction took hold. We drove to Kew Hospital and rang the back door buzzer. No answer. We rang again, still no answer.

'What's going on?' I asked as another contraction took hold.

'Beats me.' Peter was becoming edgy. 'I'll break the door down if they don't come soon.' We rang again, still no answer.

'Do we call an ambulance just to get into this hospital?' Peter was beginning to shout.

'Press again, and if they don't come, we may have to go through Emergency.' We rang again, this time we heard footsteps. The door opened. 'Oh!' said the surprised looking nurse as she let us in. 'I am really sorry.

We thought it was an April fool's joke. We have been playing practical jokes most of the night and thought this was one too.' Considering it was the 1st of April, I could see their point. We were ushered into a room, and the nurse rang the doctor. He monitored my progress, but as I walked into the hospital, the contractions ceased.

'Well, the best thing you can do is go home and wait. It'll probably be another twenty-four hours before you're due,' the doctor informed me.

I inwardly groaned. I felt so uncomfortable and couldn't see how I could possibly last the distance. I had all the symptoms of labour except the rupturing of the water. Once we arrived home, I rang around asking people to pray for the baby to come soon. After Peter left for Discipleship Training Program (DTP), I lay down on the bed with a hot water bottle on my lower stomach. Five minutes later, my waters broke, and I immediately jumped out of bed rejoicing and yelling, 'Hallelujah'. God had answered our prayer in His mercy upon me.

I phoned Peter and Rosemary, and with Rose, we traipsed back to the hospital who were there to support me and to witness the birth. Just over three hours later, Janessa Hannah arrived, weighing 7 lb 10 oz. Wonder of wonders, my little baby girl was finally here. Janessa, which comes from the name Jane, means God is gracious. I kept looking at the crib she was lying in, staring constantly at the pink nappy pins on the side. I could hardly believe my eyes even though God had told me four and a half years ago I would have a girl.

When we brought Janessa home from the hospital, Rose and her husband Bob had arrived. We sat in the lounge room discussing the miracle of Janessa's conception and birth and agreed to pray that she would have a sister also. How amazing God is! He was with me all the way, holding my hand, throughout it all.

During the next few weeks, we received congratulations from many people over the birth of our daughter. I agreed with them completely of course but it seemed like there was something missing in my heart. I struggled with breastfeeding. I felt Holy Spirit prompting me to go to the church to write down a prayer request on their care 'n' share sheet. I reluctantly obeyed. The following day, I had an afternoon nap, and upon wakening, I felt I needed to go and see the pastor.

The next day, I was taking a shower when this Scripture popped into my head:

'Or what man is there of you, whom if his son ask bread, will he give him a stone? Or if he ask a fish, will he give him a serpent? If you then, being evil, know how to give good gifts to your children, how much more shall your Father which is in heaven give good things to them that ask him?' (Matt. 7: 9–11).

I had asked my Heavenly Father for a daughter, which had been a very deep desire in my heart, and, here she was. I was feeling so overwhelmed that God had answered my prayer, I could hardly receive the gift. It was almost too much.

All my life, I believed that I was only worth second best and now God had given me the best (besides Jesus, of course). My sons were gifts from God, and I loved them dearly, but I had a deep longing and need for a daughter of my own. I just could not fully comprehend it all.

The next day, I went and saw Stuart and his wife Jacinta, who was also pregnant. For an hour, deep prayer was made as generational curses were broken off, another way of saying spiritual bondage, which had passed down from one generation to another affecting me today had been cut off. Now I could understand why my relationship with my own mother had been so dysfunctional; she was like an older sister than a mother. She had a distanced and dysfunctional relationship with her mother. So how could I be a functional mother with my daughter if I only knew the dysfunctional relationship of a mother and daughter?

It all made sense. Up to that point, there had been no bonding between my daughter and me, due to no fault of my own, but a disconnection. This was broken off; my daughter and I bonded. Praise God. I was in the right place at the right time, and God knew I needed to be living at Hawthorn at that exact time.

Life went along just fine. Around the time Janessa was nine months old, I had a dream that I had given birth to a baby girl. A few days later, I had given birth to another baby girl, and all I could see was a pair of long, slender legs growing and growing.

I conceived again. By this time, Peter had completed the DTP. Rose and I were booked in for the following year. It was arranged that Peter would look after Janessa while I did the Program. We planned to have another baby the year after, but God's timing was sooner than we'd anticipated. Meanwhile, I took my hat off to Peter who allowed me to attend the program and became Mr Mum to all our children for two days a week.

I had a few minutes of quiet time, when I was a few weeks pregnant, which was a rare occasion at best. I had been extremely tired with the lead-up to Christmas and the New Year. I sat down to pray. My thoughts went to our baby, the boys, and then to Peter. I was reminded of the promise God had given me: *I was to have a daughter too,* but this time, softly, in my spirit, it was as if He said, *I was to have a daughter two*. God was confirming to me that this child would also be a girl in answer to the prayer we had prayed when Janessa was brought home from hospital, even giving me the dream.

Once again, I struggled, accepting the timing of the pregnancy. It didn't fit in with my idea. God knew better, and I had grown to the point spiritually to lay all such silly thoughts of rejection completely aside.

First day of DTP finally arrived. 'Hi boys! Sharon?' Rose called out as she walked through the front door. The children were getting ready for school.

The boys mumbled something back.

'Put the kettle on, Rose, I won't be long,' I called out from the bedroom. Peter was running around organising Janessa so he could work at home repairing radios and televisions while Janessa slept. Radio and television parts were part and parcel of our home decor. The boys said goodbye and headed out the door for school, which was a block away. The neighbourhood was full of children heading to school, so we had no hesitation about them meeting up with their friends and walking to school. 'How was the traffic?' I heard Peter say to Rose.

'Hectic. I left Bob to get the kids ready for school and left early. Otherwise, I wouldn't be here now. Melbourne traffic is bumper to bumper if you leave a few minutes late.'

'Don't we know that?' Peter had learnt to judge the timing to leave for work too.

'Glad you came early, Rose,' I said as I entered the kitchen. We chattered about the kids and the weekend. Then Rose and I left Peter with Janessa and walked down the road to the church.

'Grab yourselves a name badge and find your folders on the table just inside the door,' said the woman at the desk as she ticked us off the roster.

'It's like going back to school.' Rose laughed.

'Know what you mean,' I replied while looking around to see if I knew anyone. A few I knew quite well, and others, I hadn't met before. We mingled while introducing ourselves.

'Ok, everyone take a seat,' Ben said after he arrived and put down some books on the front table. The tables had been arranged in a square so we could see each other. He introduced himself and continued to explain some of the first-term's agenda. We then had to introduce ourselves. Our group was much smaller than Peter's the year before. I absolutely thrived spiritually and felt incredibly blessed.

As the weeks went by, my stomach grew rapidly, and at ten weeks, I could feel a sensation like a pushing down upon my cervix of the tiny baby pressing inside. It was school holidays, so we headed down to Phillip Island to catch up with friends and family, and I took Janessa for a walk down the main street of Cowes in her pram. At the main intersection, I ran into my best friend Fiona and her two older daughters who were bouncing around excitedly bursting with their news. 'Sharon, am I glad to see you. I can't wait to tell you my good news. Guess what! I'm pregnant,' she gushed, doting on baby Janessa.

'What, that's amazing! I'm having another baby too. Tell me, when are you due?'

'Twenty-third September.'

'Can't be. That's when I'm due!' I exclaimed, as we hugged each other. 'Wouldn't it be wonderful if we were in hospital together?'

At the end of the pregnancy, I was huge. I was much larger than I had been with any of my other pregnancies. With Janessa, I had been quite small. I found it tiring carrying around all the extra weight, as I was thirty-eight years old with a toddler as well as three sons going or about to go through adolescence. I booked into two hospitals for the birth; the first being St. George Hospital at Kew where I had given birth to Janessa (in case I went earlier), and the second in Cowes as we would be down on Phillip Island for the school holidays. I was utterly frightened of going through the labour again because it was so soon after the last one. I hadn't forgotten the details.

School holidays arrived, so we packed the car and drove back to Phillip Island where we stayed with Peter's mother. Because of my size, feeling uncomfortable, and having to move around the bed frequently, Peter decided to move into the spare bedroom. Thomas was at camp while Grant was at his aunt and uncle's place on the farm. My due date arrived and departed with not even a twinge. A few days later, I woke at 6 a.m. with a hind water leak and contractions. 'How far apart are they?' Peter asked concerned.

'Ten minutes so far,' I said feeling calm. I now had peace.

'What do you want to do? Go now and see what they say or wait?' Peter was getting anxious and looked as if he wanted to cart me to the hospital.

'Let's wait for a while and see how it goes.' I was surprised to have such peace over the impending labour. Nothing happened throughout the day, so I walked to bring things on a little quicker. 'We should go now, Peter,' I said calmly, early in the evening. We phoned the hospital and then drove in. The doctor examined me; I was only 4 centimetres dilated. 'Fiona is here with her baby girl. Why not go and see her?' I enthused.

We walked down the corridor to her room. Fiona was holding her daughter. Looking up and smiling, she said, 'Isn't she beautiful?' She was.

We fussed over and praised Fiona and her daughter until the nurse came in and escorted Peter and me into the labour room. The doctor ruptured the fore-waters, and away I went in earnest with contractions coming closer together.

The nurse on duty that night in this little country bush nursing hospital was excellent. She had three children of her own and anticipated every need. Peter and I had rung around to many of our Christian friends asking for them to pray for me during the labour, so I felt reassured and at peace that all would go well. I was listening to Christian instrumental music through my headphones when I felt something expel from me. We looked on the pad, and there was meconium, which meant the baby had poohed inside me and was in distress. The nurse gave me an anxious look. The hospital had recently lost a baby. 'I'm calling the doctor now.' And she hurried out the door.

The doctor arrived a few minutes later. 'We need to organise an air helicopter in case you have to be transferred to the mainland.'

'If I sit on the toilet, it may help to dilate the cervix more.' They didn't stop me. So I went and sat on the toilet.

Shorter than what the doctor expected, at 10 p.m., our second baby girl, Kayley Elizabeth, was born. She weighed 9 pounds. It was 28 September 1994. Kayley, like her brother Jethro, was born with the cord around her hand, up against her cheek, around her neck – just as a woman from DTP had given a word of knowledge to me. As she was coming out, he noticed that her colour was not right, so he quickly pulled her out and then cut the cord, which caused blood to spatter all over the wall behind him.

I waited to hear her cry, but she didn't, not at all like my other babies when they'd been born. I became anxious and wanted to go and see what was happening. Was she alive? Was something terribly wrong? With a wash of relief, I heard her cry. Holding her was wonderful. I checked her over and noticed a roll of fat behind her neck and on her knees. I had never seen this before in any of my babies, so it delighted me. She was different to Janessa and had little hair with these long fingers and toes like her brother Jethro.

Thomas was fourteen, Grant twelve, Jethro nine, and Janessa eighteen months old.

Peter and I had not been able to agree upon a name until I was twenty-six weeks pregnant. I sensed Kayley to be a Jewish name. We called into a bank on the way back from holidays, and the bank teller's name was Caley. Upon getting back in the car, I asked Peter if he liked that name, and he did. It is actually the nickname to the Jewish name Kehlilah which means crown or laurel. There was no room for me in the small hospital, so I was put in a spare bed in the two-bed ward next to an elderly man who was coughing while in the process of dying. Being all pumped up after having just given birth, I couldn't stop thinking about the delivery and was unable to sleep, so I rang the nurse. 'I really can't settle. Is there anywhere else I could go?' I asked when the nurse came in.

'You could go in the lounge room. There is a chair that lays out into a bed. It is quite comfy, and you could watch TV for a while to relax.' So I was moved into the lounge.

The next day, I was given the best hospital room in the place (I was a public patient). This was a private room with its own bathroom and toilet. How good is God? My room was next door to Fiona's, and we had such a great time being there together; again, answered prayer. It was truly a blessed time for both of us, and our daughters are still friends today.

Our two baby girls were in the nursing room together side-by-side asleep. Visitors could view them through the glass wall. My dear mother-in-law Jean came to visit and began cooing over Fiona's daughter Laura thinking that this was her granddaughter. I absolutely cracked up, tears flowing down my cheeks in hysterics. Instead of the fourth day blues, I had the fourth day laughter.

I was discharged on day four because we had to get back to Hawthorn. How times had changed since having Thomas! I was discharged after twelve days with him and day four with Kayley. It was actually much better to get home earlier rather than later, back into my own familiar environment where I felt relaxed and at home.

I returned to the DTP class the week after having my baby, carrying baby in tow. One of the women in our group told me to look up Psalm 139 and read it, welcoming not only the baby into the world but also myself. I read it and it didn't hit any resounding chords in me. Then she told me to read it again. I read it again, and this time I wept. This is for you too, dear reader:

> *'O Lord, you have searched me, and known me. You know my down sit- ting and my uprising, you understand my thought afar off. You compass my path and my lying down, and are acquainted with all my ways. For there is not a word in my tongue, but, lo, O Lord, you know it altogether. You have beset me behind and before, and laid your hand upon me. Such knowledge is too wonderful for me; it is high, I cannot attain unto it. Whither shall I go from your spirit? Or whither shall I flee from your presence? If I ascend up into heaven, you are there: if I make my bed in hell, behold, you are there. If I take the wings of the morning, and dwell in the uttermost parts of the sea; even there shall your hand lead me, and your right hand shall hold me. If I say, Surely the darkness shall cover me; even the night shall be light about me. Yes, the darkness hides not from you; but the night shines as the*

> *day: the darkness and the light are both alike to you. For you have pos- sessed my reins: you have covered me in my mother's womb. I will praise you; for I am fearfully and wonderfully make: marvellous are your works; and that my soul knows right well. My substance was not hid from you, when I was made in secret, and curiously wrought in the lowest parts of the earth. Your eyes did see my substance, yet being imperfect; and in your book all my members were written, which in continuance were fashioned, when as yet there was none of them. How precious also are your thoughts unto me, O God! How great is the sum of them! If I should count them, they are more in number than the sand: when I awake, I am still with you.' (Ps. 139: 1–18, KJV)*

Oh, how great is the love of the Father unto us! He loves you and me so much, far more than we can ever understand or comprehend, but now, here in my arms, was living proof of His great love for me. I had two tiny daughters and three strong sons who were living proof of His great and mighty love towards me and my husband and He answers prayer. Every baby conceived and each and every person is evidence of the Father's great gift of life. Every person is unique and special to Him. It is totally unfathomable.

At that moment, I accepted myself and believed what God's Word said about me through the experience of my personal relationship with Him. The self-rejection I had experienced in the past was being loosened off me. How freeing!

CHAPTER 14

Surely he hath borne our griefs, and carried our sorrows: yet we did esteem him stricken, smitten of God, and afflicted. (Isa. 53: 4, KJV)

HALFWAY THROUGH 1994, I BELIEVED God revealed to me that He was calling us to return to Phillip Island at the end of the year. One day, it seemed to me as though the letters 'Phillip Island' were superimposed in capital letters in the sky. 'Do you think we should go back to the Island, Peter?' I asked not really sure if that is where Peter wanted to go even though I believed God had shown me we were to go back.

'I am sure we are, but I love it here and would like to stay for another year.' Peter had settled and really enjoyed the friendship and male companionship he received in Hawthorn.

'Have you prayed about it?'

'Mmm. I think I will talk to Ben and see what he thinks,' Peter replied after a few minutes of debating. We spoke to the pastor who said he would pray about it, and later, he too confirmed that he believed that it was to be so. Kayley was three months old and Janessa twenty-one months when they were dedicated to the Lord. I could feel a strong resistance going on in the spiritual realm like I was coming up against a wall of resistance and turmoil, as though the very atmosphere was chaotic and all abuzz, but we pushed through, and our girls were prayed over at the church. We now yielded willingly to His will, even delighting in His will for His Name's sake. We had learnt by now that God is pleased when we pray specifically, so we prayed. 'Lord, we need a five-bedroom house with a bath, a garage, and fully fenced.'

Soon afterwards, I had a phone call from Fiona. 'Friends of mine have to move and want to rent their house out. It is huge and would suit your family. It's in Cowes just off the main road. I can organise for you to look through it if you want.'

'Really! We will be down on the weekend. Do you think we can go through it then?'

'I'll let you know.' She hung up.

We were delighted. When we drove up to the house, we knew it was the place for us. It was the house we had been praying for – in fact, it was a two-storey with six bedrooms. The boys raced around checking every nook and cranny and then chose which rooms they wanted; they were as excited as we were. The position was perfect, a quiet street where the boys could ride their bikes and play cricket and close to the shops and school.

We moved back to Phillip Island after I had finished my DTP, which was in line with the Christmas school holidays, and settled into the large house. The boys absolutely loved moving back to be close to their friends and relatives. Even so I had a sense of foreboding, wondering in the back of my mind if the place would take a heavy toll on our marriage.

Life on the Island settled into a normal pace though at times I felt overwhelmed. Maybe it was because I had a lot going on in my home life with our large family, what with it being a mixture of teenagers and toddlers.

Peter worked extremely hard, once again in partnership with Will, putting in everything he had, as well as immersing himself in the local cricket so he could coach our sons, which took up a lot of his spare time and energy. Quality time with each other was slipping away.

'Do you want to go to the camp or not?' I asked when Peter and I were finally alone after another busy day. We had been invited to a church camp with all our old friends from Hawthorn along with other Christians from differing denominations.

'We can't afford the four weeks. I don't know. It would be good to catch up with the Hawthorn mob. We could go for the first two weeks as it will be a quiet time at work.'

'The boys will have school holidays then too, so they won't miss out on school,' I said, working days out on the calendar.

'You sort it out. I'll let Will know tomorrow,' Peter said.

Our girls came down with runny noses and coughs the day we left for camp. The weather was very cold. Janessa's cough progressively worsened, so we bought some new, strong cough medicine which recently had come out on the market.

Lancefield is a beautiful part of Victoria, and the camp was set in amongst the bush. It had an open field where people could play football and a dam in the distance. The sleeping quarters were a long building with bedrooms at both ends and a communal meeting room in the middle. We checked on the notice board to see where our room was. Each family was allocated a room to sleep in.

I grabbed the esky which had Janessa's medicine in it plus a suitcase and went into our room. We unpacked the bags and settled the sleeping arrangements for the boys and Janessa. I put the esky underneath Kayley's port-a-cot; we then went across the walkway to the kitchen and dining room facilities. We were greeted like long-lost friends. It was a joy to catch up while having a hot drink and home-made biscuits. Then, we headed into the meeting room.

Two God-fearing men, David, a world renowned Bible teacher, spoke first, then John, and then David once again, then John; this continued all throughout their message. Each time, the message was different but, strangely, they interrelated to what the other had spoken earlier.

The teaching had been building up all week, and it was powerful; however, we were all very tired. At the end of the first week, I woke up still feeling tired and exhausted. It was 7.20 a.m., and Janessa, now two years old, had woken up before me and climbed out of her bed. I groaned and then rolled over not wanting to leave my comfortable bed. 'Mummy,' Janessa said, shaking me.

'Play with your toys. I'll get up in a few minutes.' Peter and the boys were still asleep. They were as tired as I was. I fell back to sleep. I woke with a start. Janessa was quietly playing with her toys; Kayley was gurgling to herself in her cot. Peter was up, while the boys were nowhere in sight.

'The boys have gone for breakfast. We let you sleep a bit longer,' Peter explained. I slowly climbed out of bed and went for a shower. The water was hot and refreshing. Peter was still in the bedroom when I came back; Kayley and Janessa were dressed and ready for the day. I picked up the esky to get Janessa's medicine, but the bottle wasn't there.

'Have you seen Janessa's medicine?' I asked Peter.

'It's in the esky,' he replied not aware that I had picked it up.

'No, it's not. Did you take it out earlier?' Peter turned, knelt down, and felt under it and then stood up with the bottle in his hand. It was nearly empty. We both looked at Janessa. Neither of us noticed the slight colouring of her lips, the colour of the medicine. She had drunk almost the whole bottle.

I was utterly horrified! 'What shall we do? Call a doctor, call the poisons line, or take her to the hospital? Lord, what do we do?'

'Don't panic, Sharon. Let's just see what happens. There is little we can do now anyway.' Peter was calmer than I had ever seen him in a situation like this. We headed off to the kitchen. Janessa staggered down the hallway as if she was drunk. Once in the kitchen, I kept a close eye on her while we had breakfast, and soon after, she vomited up a lot of the medicine. We all gathered together for prayer in the meeting room, and when the pastor prayed 'in Jesus's Name' at the end of the prayer, Janessa again vomited up the rest of the medicine that was in her system. In the dining area, some of the adults minded the children for the parents who attended the meetings. I left Janessa with them explaining to them what had just happened yet being strangely at peace in the midst of it all.

It had been snowing outside, and I remember gazing out at the cars parked, snow all over them, feeling that I was different to everybody else. I could not fathom why.

At the meeting that day, David spoke quietly to the group in the hall. 'Wait quietly upon the Lord and ask him to reveal a situation where someone may have brought shame upon you or where you had brought shame upon them.'

Don't be ridiculous, no one had brought shame on me or vice versa, I thought. I was rather blasé thinking that the Holy Spirit wasn't going to show me anything. I closed my eyes anyway and prayed.

I immediately got a picture of a swimming pool, and then my memory jogged. When my sister and I had lived with my aunt and uncle for six months with my grandmother whilst waiting for our father to arrive from New Zealand, their English neighbour, a man in late middle-age, had offered to take Rose and I to the pool. I was nine, nearly ten years old. It can be hot in Brisbane, so swimming is a favourite pastime. He would swim with us. He used to hug me at the side of the pool and caress my newly developing little breasts. I had completely forgotten all about this. SHAME broke off me. It was like I had seen the world through different-coloured glasses before from everybody else. I cried and cried and cried for at least half an hour. My world from that incident right up to the present had been covered in a coat of shame, and I did not even know it until then. I was now set free from it.

I tried to take a hold of myself and made my way back to the dining room where Peter was having lunch holding our baby daughter Kayley. Reflecting back to the time when I suspected I had conceived a baby, I recall praying that she would look like me. Since having her, I had secretly thought she was an unattractive baby, which had been a lie; a reflection of how I had come to see myself, but now that the shame had lifted and I set my eyes on her again. I realised that she had the most beautiful blue eyes and blonde fluffy hair. Kayley was amazingly long. I imagined how tall and gracious she would become. Kayley's hands were amazing – she had the longest fingers. I started to believe that she'd have a firm grip on this world and through her hands much would be achieved.

I had been delivered from a stronghold. This stronghold was called SHAME. It was a door where the devil had access to me. Now free, I was onto the next level of new beginnings and deeper faith. No longer broken inside – I was healed and restored through the victory won for me through Jesus's death on the cross. He takes all our sins, all our grief and sorrow, all our shame, and all our infirmities (physically, mentally, and emotionally) and exchanges them on the cross for His righteousness, His cleansing, His peace, and His healing.

Three months later, I attended a prayer ministry school, again at the Lancefield camp. This time, I was on my own to do business with God. It was also at the time of Kayley's first birthday, so it was at a cost for me to go, but I knew the Lord wanted me there. Peter graciously took care of our children.

I had been in many 'no-go' areas during my life, particularly during my later teen years. I had seen a clairvoyant, gone to a spiritualist church, had my fortune read by tarot cards, had tea-leaves read to me, had my palm read, had a birth chart lined up with horoscopes, etc, etc. My father had told me about some of these things which were wrong, but I had rebelled and gone my own way. Influenced by a friend concerning 'new age', I had my wedding ring swung over my pregnant stomach on a piece of my hair to determine what sex the baby would be, gone for acupuncture, visited a hypnotist, and so forth. The list is exhaustive. Some of these things I did even ignorantly as a Christian. I felt like I carried a huge weight on my back and shoulders. Even though I willingly went to this prayer ministry school, my flesh screamed to run.

A Christian brother and sister took me through the list. There was another person in the corner of the room praying for me as well as other Christians transacting with God in other rooms while another group of brothers and sisters in Christ prayed as the Holy Spirit led them to, in the dining room. Six hours later, my session was finished. The heavy sack of guilt that I had been carrying around has now been lifted completely off me. It was a huge relief.

We had been so incredibly blessed through our association with the church in Hawthorn that we found it difficult to find another church on Phillip Island to be a part of, so we therefore began a house church in our own home with our long-time friends Pat and George and another younger couple with their daughter. We would share a meal together, read the Bible, and pray. An older pastor and his wife, friends of Pat and George's, would attend at times also.

When Kayley was eighteen months old, I decided to become a Family Day Carer taking pre-school children into my home. Because I already had two pre-schoolers, I could only care for two other children. I chose to do this twice a week, and sometimes, if arranged, one of them might sleep over. On one of those days, I cared for Fiona's daughter. I formed a friendship with one of the single mums who needed a break from her two younger children, and I was able to lead her to the Lord. We all felt connected. I relished this time. Small children are so delightful in their innocence and bring great joy. However, my marriage with Peter was beginning to slip.

Peter had waited a long time to purchase a computer knowing that they were being constantly updated and replaced. The time had now come, just before Christmas, for the long awaited computer, CD Rom, and printer to arrive. This was Peter's forte, the fascinating world of technology, back in 1996. When I first met Peter, his job was classified as a Radio Tradesman covering a broad range of electronic repairs. He is very clever in this department. He then progressed to installing pay TV and satellite dishes and, many years later, Christian television via satellite.

This new computer took pride of place in one of the bedrooms, which now became an office, and swallowed up any spare time that Peter or the boys had. Any quality time for our relationship as husband and wife or as a family unit was disregarded and put on hold. This machine, or rather technology, became an obvious idol in our home, and Peter seemed, as it were, to sit at the feet of it to worship it – well, that's how I perceived it.

At the same time that the computer came into our home, I was suffering from a urinary tract infection. I had never had one before, and I put off visiting the doctor. It felt like I was passing glass every time I went to the toilet. I felt like I was going under, as if a big black cloud was over me and I sensed such utter despair.

Everything was getting the better of me – I thought I would pull out a bottle of red wine to drown my sorrows and I would ring my friend Rosemary to pour my heart out to. I had stopped drinking alcohol when I was a Seventh-Day-Adventist but gradually the occasional alcoholic drink or two came back into my life. It was now late at night, and I talked on the phone for over a couple of hours, unwell, and in emotional turmoil. I drank the whole bottle on my own.

The next morning, I woke up and did not feel too well at all. Any wonder. I now had diarrhoea whilst my body tried to rid itself of too much alcohol in the system – it was like a hangover but much worse. I stayed in bed. As the morning wore on, I realised that my breathing had changed and I could only take short breaths. I was so grieved in my heart to the point of being overwhelmingly wretched over the condition of my marriage. All I had really wanted in life was to have a good and happy marriage and family. I knew that divorce wasn't the answer; having come from a broken home, I certainly did not want to pass that legacy on to my children, especially looking at how far we had come in the Lord. I felt trapped in circumstances beyond my control, and somehow I felt I was a victim in the middle of it.

It became harder and harder to breathe. It came to my understanding that the Lord was taking my life away, my very breath. I was dying. I knew that I did not even have time to ring for an ambulance. Holy Spirit spoke within me saying He would take me home to heaven. As a young girl, I had always wanted to go to heaven to see Jesus and be with Him. He then gave me a choice: I could go to be with Him or I could stay. I chose to stay because my two daughters were still small and needed their mother, and then I told the Lord from somewhere out of the depths of my being that I would fight for this marriage. Immediately, my breathing returned to normal. I was now totally overawed once again at just how much God loves me (not just me, but you too). When I grieve, He also feels my pain and grief. How good and gracious is our God! Later that day, my oldest son, Thomas, who was sixteen, came into the lounge where I was sitting quietly. The girls were outside playing in the sand. He sat down next to me. 'Mum?'

'Mmm,' I said and then turned to look at him. He had tears in his eyes. 'Are you all right?' I asked concerned.

'You nearly died today, Mum.' He almost sobbed. 'Yes, I know.' I acknowledged his belief.

Thomas seemed to struggle with something and then he said, 'Holy Spirit told me He was taking you home today, Mum, and I said, "No, don't take Mum. Take me. The girls are only little." He didn't take me, and you are still alive.' I hugged him in tears. Through my son, he confirmed to me that this had been very real. Thomas has a tender and sensitive heart and continues to show wonderful attributes of humility today. The Lord is truly amazing.

CHAPTER 15

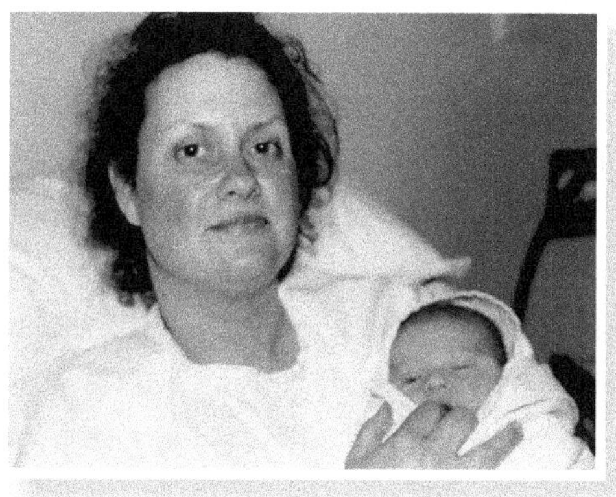

That the God of our Lord Jesus Christ, the Father of glory, may give to you the spirit of wisdom and revelation in the knowledge of him: the eyes of your understanding being enlightened. (Eph. 1: 17–18a, KJV)

I HEARD AROUND TOWN THAT an older, mature Christian couple Sally and Dan, who were strong in the Lord, were living on Phillip Island and running a Restoration Course at the Baptist church. I had previously met them and was very much drawn to them. 'It really helped me, Sharon. You wouldn't believe the difference it's made in my life,' my friend said while we were in my kitchen, talking about the Restoration Course.

'I don't know. I had prayer awhile ago and I broke off all that was blocking me. Why would I want to go do that?' I queried, having already decided against going.

'Well, there are a few people you know who are going. It really is good.'

'I suppose it won't harm.' I relinquished, so I registered for the course.

It ran for one day a week, for four weeks, and there were a number of us attending. Each topic was brought up with the last ones being on grief and grace, and the whole thing was bathed in prayer. Sally would stand at the front with her shoes off whilst she taught. Words of knowledge were given as the Holy Spirit prompted her, a supernatural revelation from God.

As they spoke on the topic of deep-rooted grief, they explained how sometimes in our lives, when we have lost a loved one, we don't allow ourselves the necessary process of acknowledging and dealing with the grief and 'stuff' all our feelings down, suppressing and cutting off our emotions to our great detriment. This then produces a blockage in our soul and spirit (our mind, will, and emotions), which shuts out the full flow of the Holy Spirit. After listening to the last session, I had a vague notion that I should speak to Sally and Dan, but they seemed to be busy, and anyway, we were enjoying a fellowship luncheon together at the end. I drove home thinking of all the things they had said over the day. I had this strange feeling, something which I couldn't put my finger on; something was bubbling up in me.

As it was a public holiday, the kids were at home, the older boys looking after their little sisters. 'Mum,' called the girls as I drove into the yard. It was always a joy to see my children playing together and watching out for each other, most of the time anyway. The girls ran out to the car and flung their arms around me as I opened the car door.

'Well, it's nice to know you missed me too,' I said, laughing. We went into the house, and the girls prattled on about their day, the boys following suit, and went straight to the fridge. All the while as I was talking and watching my children, I did not have closure in my heart; something was still stirring, and I just knew I had to go back to the church to see if Dan and Sally were still there. 'I have to go back to the meeting for a while again,'

I said as the need grew in my heart. The boys nodded and offered the girls some food they had taken out of the fridge.

I drove back down to the hall. Their car was still in the parking lot, and I quietly praised God. One of the elders of the church was tidying up. He looked up when I entered and nodded in greeting. Sally and Dan were talking quietly. I could no longer constrain myself and out flooded a torrent of pent-up grief that had been buried for twenty-five years. I fell apart at the thought of the ugly sin which I had done. 'I had an abortion when I was younger, and I know God has forgiven me, but I haven't forgiven myself.' I cried in agony at the thought of what I had done to my unborn child remembering my sister's words 'that I would regret it one day.' My heart had been hard, but now God was graciously softening it. I actually hadn't forgiven myself. All the guilt and pain and denial came pouring out like pus bursting out of an infected wound. It felt like it had been buried in the pit of my stomach all this time. I cried and cried and cried.

These precious saints prayed over me, praying that God's sweet grace, His love, and His forgiveness would flow through me. Oh, praise God for His wonderful mercy! I believe that the baby had been a little girl, a dream I'd had at the time was of a little girl standing on a veranda, and Sally also believed the baby had been a girl.

In my experience, most women I meet who have had abortions have been rejected in some measure resulting in self-rejection. Unfortunately, nowadays with some, it is also a form of contraception. If only I could go back in time and undo the greatest mistake I had ever made, but alas, I could not. She was now growing up in heaven, and I would one day meet her.

CHAPTER 16

Cast your burden upon the Lord and He will sustain you.
He will never allow the righteous to be moved. (Ps. 55: 22)

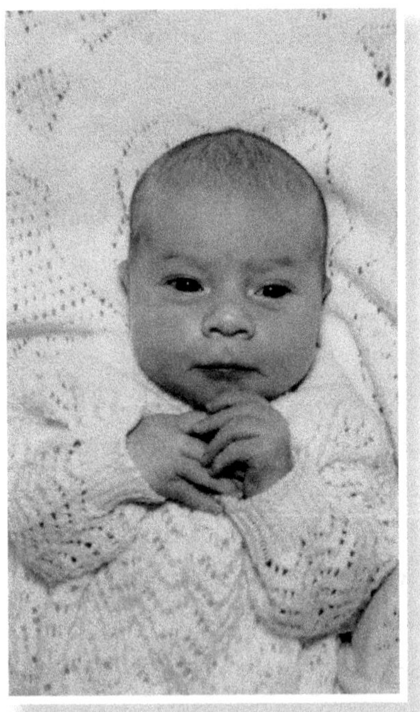

Most of the friends I was hanging around with were smokers. I hadn't smoked in twenty years, and now I found myself wanting to join them, which I foolishly did. They had many problems, and smoking was their form of coping. Every time they were feeling stressed, out would come another cigarette. It wasn't spoken, but the belief was that our problems were too large for us to handle. Smoking magnified my problems. I wanted to be like them and accepted by them. I became a social smoker when I was around these friends, and, after all, I had the problem in my marriage as it was yet again struggling to survive. My problems became a mountain which overshadowed my faith in God. I doubted God and His goodness and the seed of a lie grew, believing that my mountains were too big.

One night, God gave me a dream. I was in a house with a couple of heavy biker guys wearing black leather jackets and pants. I hopped on the back of one of the bikes with one of these dudes, and we rode off down the hill. The meaning was very plain and clear. God was warning me about the path I was taking, and it only led downhill!

I heeded God's obvious warning and stopped being in wrong agreement with my friends that our problems were too large for God to conquer. Amazingly, I did not become addicted to cigarettes again.

We loved living in our big house, but there was one problem that we found difficult to live with. The house had a flat roof and now leaked in three different areas. One leak was over Grant's bed, and the water dripped into a Tupperware celery container near his head. We informed the owners but nothing seemed to be getting done.

One day, I went shopping and had to walk from the supermarket to the chemist. I was walking past the real estate windows looking at the houses for sale and daydreaming on maybe owning one of them. On the spur of the moment, I decided I would take a look at one of the houses advertised in their window in my favourite area called Wimbledon Heights.

Returning to the car, I drove to the house advertised, and it didn't look all that inviting compared to the photo in the window. As I was turning away, I clearly heard the Holy Spirit saying to my heart that if I had a choice, which house would I choose as my home to live in. Straight away, I knew the house. I left my car where it was parked. I loved the feel of the estate and the fresh air and peace. I walked around to where this house was, right in the middle of the estate. When I arrived at the house, my heart gave an extra beat; there was a sign out the front saying 'For Private Sale' with a telephone number on it. I couldn't wait until Peter arrived home that evening.

'How would you like to live in Wimbledon Heights?' I asked Peter once the kids were settled for the night.

'Why?' Peter asked non-committed to any answer while he was typing on his computer.

'I saw a house that I think would suit us, and it is for sale.'

'We can't afford to buy anything yet. Where would we get the money?' Peter was now looking at me as if I was crazy.

'We could ask if they would be willing to rent with the view towards buying. We really need to get another house urgently.'

'What is the number?' He went to the phone and talked to the owners. 'They are open to looking at tenants as the current tenants are about to move. We can see the house on the weekend.'

I was overjoyed. It was everything I hoped for. Three bedrooms and a loft, dado boards halfway up the walls downstairs, a large spa bath in the bathroom with a large window overlooking a fernery, a wood-heater which heated up the whole house upstairs and downstairs (an answer to prayer because I did not like a cold house), and to top it all off, we could even see the bay from the balcony upstairs. It was an unusual design with lots of angles and lots of warm wood everywhere. We loved it. It was a really sweet cottage. We promptly moved in, renting it for several months before applying for a mortgage loan from the bank to buy the house, which was accepted.

We had only been in our house for six weeks when Thomas was invited to a party by a female friend of his who lived in a nearby street. It was the end of year twelve exams. Thomas was seventeen. 'I'm going to sleepover at the party tonight,' Thomas said as he headed out the door to high school.

'You didn't mention this before, Thomas. You sure you want to stay?' 'Yeah, Mum.' He left before I could say anything else. I was astonished because I knew that Thomas really enjoyed sleeping in his own bed. He hadn't previously mentioned anything about a sleepover.

I was extremely tired early that evening and went to bed at 9 p.m. praying beforehand that God would take care of my oldest son and to wake me if necessary. At midnight, I awoke to a very loud noise outside my bedroom window. I knew God had woken me just as I had prayed and that there was an angel standing guard there, a very noisy angel at that.

My first thought was Thomas, so I raced downstairs to see if he had come home only to discover he had not. I was a mother on a mission. I jumped in my car and drove around to where the house was and knocked on the door. I was going to insist that Thomas come home with me. There was no answer, so I cautiously peered in through a side window. The teenagers were in a circle on the floor, and a couple of them had passed out, either from excessive alcohol or marijuana. Something in me drew back and I thought better of just barging in there zealously. I went home frustrated and unsure of what to do next. Once inside, I rummaged through the cupboard and pulled out the telephone book to call these people, but it appeared his friend's family did not have a phone number listed. Thomas's younger brother Grant, being the night owl he was, was still up. 'I am at a loss to know what to do. Do I go in and get him out or leave him?' I confided in Grant, explaining my predicament.

'Thomas would not speak to you if you ostracised him in front of his peers, Mum,' Grant said without second thoughts.

'So now, what do I do?' I questioned more myself than Grant.

Grant shook his head. 'Good question.' And turned back to what he was doing.

I went upstairs and did the only thing I could do. I prayed boldly to God to send His angel to Thomas telling him to come home to his own bed and that Thomas would walk through the front door within the next two minutes. And that's just what Thomas did to my great delight. Hallelujah. If only I had trusted God all along and simply just asked Him in prayer. These are His children and He cares for them more than we ever possibly could. All we have to do is ask Him and He will hear and answer and send His angels to take charge over them.

My boys were going through their teenage years quickly, and I seemed to be slipping back into mine. I would occasionally drink alcohol either with my husband or my friends. It helped me to relax. However, I felt that God's desire for me was not to drink any alcohol at all. It got to the stage that even one glass of wine would go straight through me. I still continued to insist on my own way though. As the problems and stresses in my life increased, so too did my consumption of alcohol. One particular Saturday evening, I went out with a few of my single female friends and had numerous alcoholic drinks, to try and drown out my sorrows and despair in defeat. My marriage was hard. In the wee hours of the morning, I decided I had to go home. I could hardly see straight and everything around me seemed to go round in circles. I stumbled to my car and with great care drove home. To this day, I don't know how I made it safely.

I parked the car in the drive and stumbled up the steps to the front door. The kitchen light was on, but everyone was asleep. I managed to walk through the front door passing down the corridor to the bathroom. I don't remember how I fell, but the next thing I knew I was on the floor, bruising myself in the process. No one came in to see if I was all right, they must have slept through the noise. What was exceedingly difficult to bear though was the dark wall of separation I felt between myself and God. I knew in my heart that I had done wrong and would say sorry even though I knew that God had already forgiven me, yet I was weak to pull away from it.

Early one Sunday afternoon, after one of those nights out, I received visitors who were Christian friends of mine. I was still lying in bed because I had a terrible hangover and felt just awful. Then I heard footsteps coming up the steps, a knock, and then the door slowly opened. 'Sharon, can I come in?'

I peered out from under the blankets. 'Oh, Breanna!' I felt so ashamed that my friend saw me in this mess. Breanna came over and sat down on the bed next to me, placed her hand on my shoulder, and rubbed it. She wasn't there to judge or condemn me.

'Can I pray for you?' she asked, looking intently at me. 'Please' was all I could say, my tears near-to-overflowing.

She prayed, 'The spiritual hold that Satan has over you in this area of weakness is now broken.' I cried while she comforted me. We spoke for a few more minutes and then she left.

I continued to drink alcohol but only occasionally and in small quantities I now had control of it instead of the other way round. However, I could still hear the small, still voice of the Holy Spirit to totally abstain from alcohol.

CHAPTER 17

No test or temptation that comes your way is beyond the course of what others have had to face. All you remember is that God will never let you down; He'll never let you be pushed past your limit; He'll always be there to help you through it. (1 Cor. 10: 13, Msg)

As I HAVE JUST MENTIONED, my health deteriorated, and I suffered from constant indigestion and had to be careful what I ate. I went to see the doctor who required me to go have an ultrasound which revealed gallstones. This illness had been prevalent on my mother's side of the family. Gall is another word for bitterness, and I had harboured hard feelings of bitterness and resentment towards Peter over the years. I had been completely blinded to it though. The doctor said I required keyhole surgery but to wait a little while for the inflammation to settle down. I decided that I would try a natural healing remedy which was a cleansing diet to rid the body of the gallstones. I had nothing to lose, I figured. My condition this time round was worse than I had previously experienced many years ago. At times, it could only be described as glass turning round and round in my stomach. After following the health plan to rid my body of gallstones, I realised that this time it had not been completely successful. Every time I ate food with a little bit of fat in it, I would know about it. I was disappointed by this outcome and unsure of what to do next.

Two weeks went by, and I was still feeling quite unwell. One evening, I indulged myself with a few squares of chocolate before retiring to bed and afterwards chastised myself on making such an unwise decision and giving in to temptation. That night, I had the most incredible dream which I recorded in my dream journal. I will relate it to you: I was in a large hospital in a big room, like outpatients. The head doctor spoke to a group of us who were about to have the same operation to remove gallstones. I saw myself being opened up, and they found out that there was something else wrong with me. Someone in my dream gave me a Bible verse about death, which was repeated by somebody else in the dream.

When I woke up the next morning, I was completely healed! I found this verse in my Bible in Hosea 13: 14.

> *I will ransom them from the power of the grave; I will redeem them from death. O death, I will be your plagues; O grave, I will be your destruction. (Hos. 13: 14)*

In my dream, the head physician was Jesus, and He healed me of this sickness. Illness and sickness is not God's will for us. It does not belong to life or is any part of life – it belongs to death and is a part of death.

At this particular stage of my life's journey, I was forty-four years old. I had returned home with Peter several months and life was moving along. I enquired about a course in Melbourne where I could learn the skills of telephone counselling with Right to Life. Because of my own experience, I had a passion to defend the lives of innocent as-yet unborn babies who could not speak up for themselves. I did not know that at the very time I rang, they were about to commence a counselling course at an East Melbourne hospital. I decided I would attend and that I would catch the 6 a.m. bus to get to the city on time.

Well, around the exact time I began this course, I fell unexpectedly pregnant (somehow). The alarm went off very early in the morning so I could catch the 6 a.m. bus, which would take three hours for me to arrive within the heart of the city. When the alarm set turned the radio on, the song I awoke to was one I had never heard before, 'Be careful what you're dreaming of, you might go and get it,' and in an uncanny way, right then, I knew that I was pregnant. I absolutely loved babies and was fully aware that each one was a special gift from God. I had one problem…

Peter and I, one night, were discussing things, and he warned me that I was not to get pregnant. He even implied that if I ever did, he would consider leaving. I understood that he was stretched to full capacity with his quiver already full (with caring for our five children). Two weeks after I had listened to the song on the radio, my oldest daughter Janessa told me that she had dreamt I was pregnant but nobody knew about it. I really pay attention to the dreams of children. God speaks loudly and clearly to them. They don't have as much interference on their wavelength to God as we grown-ups have. A few days later, I decided to take a home test. It came out positive. I was excited yet dreading to see the result, all at the same time. I knew I could not tell Peter. At least not yet.

The following weekend, we celebrated Kayley's sixth birthday overnight in a beautiful hotel overlooking a lake close to the city. We had come to the city to go to a Hi-5 children's concert during school holidays. After we had put the girls to bed, I sat in the bath feeling distressed because I had not told Peter about the pregnancy. I finally realised that this was not good for me or the baby and that Peter had a right to know, so I broke the news to him. As I had anticipated – not well. It was a nightmare, and his negativity had a very bad effect upon me. I felt as though he was not just rejecting our baby, but me also. He was also responsible for bringing a life into the world, not just me. I had to get away and grabbed the car keys to go and visit a friend who lived not far away. We did not tell anybody about our news.

Two or three weeks later, we went to visit our oldest son Thomas who was still living in Hawthorn in Melbourne, and he related the dream he had just had. In his dream, he was pushing a baby in a pram along a path when all of a sudden a helicopter came down and snatched the baby. Thomas had no idea at all that I was even pregnant. It's incredible that the God of the Bible still speaks to us to this present today through dreams, preparing me in this case for what lay ahead and revealing mysteries to me.

Peter had by now become accustomed to the idea of another baby. I was now nine weeks pregnant, and I had put off seeing my local doctor. I now made a visit, and the doctor wanted me to have lots of tests due to my age. I did not agree to all of them, only the blood tests and the ultrasound. It was Monday, and the ultrasound was booked for the following Friday. As the day rolled around, it turned out that Peter was able to accompany me for the ultrasound because, on one of his rare days, there was no work. Praise God he did. I had prayed he would come with me.

We arrived at radiology, and the female technician tried her best to get a picture of the baby because it was such an early stage. She then blurted out coldly that the baby had no heartbeat. No compassion at all, just very matter-of-factly. We were both shocked. Nothing like this had ever happened to us before. I was in sheer disbelief.

I went back to see the doctor again, and he said how sorry he was. I told him I wanted a second ultrasound to get another opinion. I was not bleeding or cramping or anything. I believed that God could bring life back to that little heart, and I rang my sister to ask for their church to pray.

A few days later, I went to a different radiology, and the male technician was sensitive and caring (he had a heart), but the result was still the same. It was classified as a missed abortion. My body did not want to let go. Apparently the baby had stopped growing at 7½ weeks, the exact time that I had terminated my very first pregnancy.

Three days later, I began to finally bleed. I had to see a different doctor about having a curette. The theatre was being renovated, and the earliest I could get in was four days later. It was ridiculous. The next morning, the blood had turned black, and the following day, I was having full-on contractions. Peter drove me back to the doctor's, and he was ready to bop them one, seeing me in so much pain. I needed a curette urgently. I was booked in for 1 p.m. that afternoon. Peter had work to do in the area, so I sat in the car. The contractions eased a little, but I still had to breathe through them. Peter had another job a little out of town, and he wasn't sure whether he should do it or not. It would not take long. I urged him to do it. Well, the job took a lot longer than anticipated and time was ticking very fast. I now became agitated. It was 12.30 p.m., and we were meant to be at the hospital half an hour before surgery. We were ten to fifteen minutes away. Jumping into the driver's seat, I beeped the horn and turned the work vehicle and trailer around, all set to go without him. He came out, and it was 12.40 p.m. when we arrived at the hospital. I ran in apologising profusely at our delay. They had already called out my name to go down to theatre. In the end, it all turned out well because I had no time to think about things. Before I knew it, I was whipped down by trolley to have a curette by general anaesthetic and just as quick it seemed, I was whipped out again. I was out of hospital by 4 p.m.

I mulled over things a few weeks later, thinking what had it all been about. To me, it was as if a curse had been operating in my life. We had Derek Prince's book called *Blessings and Curses* and, after flicking through it, I asked God what had really happened. I believed that the Holy Spirit revealed to me that the baby's purpose in its very short life had been fulfilled and that I had never forgiven the doctor who had performed the abortion on me. I had no idea.

I grieved over the loss of this precious little life that had been given to me so briefly. This little one was also now growing up in heaven. God, in His mercy, before I knew that the baby's heartbeat had stopped, had given me a dream. I had dreamt that another woman and I were cleaning the ladies' toilets. In each cubicle, there were plastic bags for women to use when menstruating. The other woman (who looked just like the large angel in the television series *Touched by an Angel*) was swabbing the blood on this small machine. There had been an abortion, and a photo showed up of this child from the DNA. The photo was of a six-year-old girl with long blonde hair and a handsome face. She had a square chin, and she looked very much like my youngest daughter Kayley. I believe God in his grace gave me a picture of what my child looked like, and this gave me peace later on.

About a month later, after I had lost the baby, I was walking along the beach in Cowes and a willie wagtail bird kept flying alongside me as I walked along the shoreline. I questioned God, asking Him in my thoughts, what was the bird doing? I heard, again in my thoughts, a Voice like the sound of many rushing waters,

'and His voice as the sound of many waters' (Rev. 1: 15),

'You are blessed of the Lord, my child'. The bird was now opening and closing its beak, and again I enquired of the Lord what the bird was trying to tell me. Again I heard, 'He is speaking of My love for you.' The bird then flew off.

CHAPTER 18

For whatever one sows that he will also reap. (Gal. 6: 7b, KJV)

One evening, while I was clearing up after the kids were in bed, Peter and I decided together that his workaholic lifestyle pattern needed to be broken. 'Why don't we move to Tiara?' I suggested. 'Queensland has jobs going. Rose and Bob are doing really well up there. You could work on the mines.

Thomas is in Hawthorn working at McDonald's, and Grant's moving out to rent a flat in Cowes. It would give us the break we need.'

Peter looked up surprised. 'Do you want to move?'

'Yes, just for twelve months. I miss Rose and Bob since they moved. It would be good for our relationship.' Rose and Bob left Victoria a few years ago and moved to Tiara where Bob worked dredging for the mines. 'Well, you could install satellite TV on homes or put up aerials if you really want to. Tiara isn't that big. We could rent out the house here and that will cover the mortgage.'

'Let me think and pray about it.' The value of our marriage and our family took precedence over the excessive work treadmill Peter had been on and we needed a year of 'rest', so my friend Michelle agreed to rent our house while we were away.

Peter, Jethro in year eleven, and the girls, and I moved to Tiara in 2001. Peter worked manually, but it was a break from the mental stress and pressure of his previous sub-contracting work. We even had the opportunity of mini holidays as we learnt to relax and unwind. We learnt not to take life so seriously and how to have fun as a family, how to laugh and enjoy life.

I was thrilled when our two older sons came up to visit us on 11 September 2001. They turned up with wigs on their heads to surprise us. 'How was the trip?' I asked as I hugged them.

'Glad to be here. It's a long way, but we had a great time coming through.' Thomas and Grant drove up sharing the drive.

'Hi, boys, you made good time,' Peter said as he came out of the caravan greeting them, smiling. We went inside, and the boys chattered about the drive up and what they did and saw.

'Want anything up the street?' they asked heading out the door. 'No.'

When they came back, they brought in a slab of beer each for their sta in Tiara. I was horrified to see them in the same trap I had been in, in the past. That evening, we went over to the local drinking place at the bowls club. I wandered over to the bar to spend some time with my boys. What horrified me was to see my boys drinking copious amounts of alcohol, then the 9/11 attack and destruction, and me thinking I needed to order wine so that I could relate to my boys. I came home to see a television report relaying the horrific news of events emerging in New York of a plane crashing into one of the twin towers. I looked transfixed as I saw the tower collapsing. The next day, when the enormity of 9/11 sank in, I made a vow there and then to fully stop drinking alcohol.

Again, another outburst of Peter's hot temper, and I began to doubt what God had done and went running to the pastor in tears. He said to me one of the most important phrases I had ever heard in my life which was 'Sharon, you are *not* a victim!' I needed to hear those words which set me free yet again. The victory is won in Jesus.

Middle of December 2001, we celebrated an early Christmas with Rose and Bob and their family before farewelling them to return back to our home once again on Phillip Island to start life over. Our tenant and friend had moved out earlier than anticipated, and our house was left vacant, so it was imperative we return. I eagerly anticipated meeting up with our two older sons Thomas and Grant and being a complete family again.

19 November 2003, our twenty-sixth wedding anniversary, Peter and I went to a special guesthouse which was absolutely beautiful. It was owned and run by our son Grant's friend's parents. There was an indoor swimming pool, and Peter and I and Murray's parents sat in the nearby spa. Murray offered to get his mother a drink consisting of half orange juice and half wine and offered one to me as well. I declined saying that I did not drink. He kept on insisting saying, 'That one won't hurt'. Eventually, I gave in seeing as this was a special occasion. One turned to two, and then we had a delicious meal served on the huge wooden country table. Peter, who drinks alcohol on the rare occasion, had brought along a special communion wine that a friend of his had made from cherries. It was offered to me, and I accepted. It was the smoothest wine I had ever tried.

The *drought* had now broken. Two nights later, I went to a friend's place because I had been invited to a make-up party. Alcohol flowed freely, and again, it was offered to me. I accepted once again. I had a total of five large wine glasses as I empathised with my friend's daughter over the troubles she had (not a good influence on my part).

I went home that night and fell into a sound sleep. I then had a strong vision around 3 in the morning. It was so real – more real than real. I was in a room near the gates of heaven, and there were other people around me. There was an angel nearby and also a table with an open book and written on it was the year I was born and the year I died. I did not see the year. The message was very clear though. I had broken the vow I had made with the Lord to abstain from alcohol until the wedding supper of the Lamb. This was a very serious warning. The next thing that came to my mind was two Scripture verses. As a Christian who reads God's Word, I love it when the right Scripture comes to mind. These verses were fresh, and I really needed to hear this. This was God's way of communicating with me through His Word and His Holy Spirit. The first verse that came to my mind was, 'For to whomsoever much is given, of him shall be much required' (Luke 12: 48), and then instantly, 'My grace is sufficient for you: for my strength is made perfect in weakness' (2 Cor. 12: 9).

I just want to thank my Lord Jesus for His Word, His Love for me, and His mercies which are new every morning. I do not know where I'd be if it was not for 'My Master's Hand', watching, moulding, guiding, and forgiving me.

The following day, I went around to my friend's house and told her to pass on my apologies to her daughter for the way in which I had drunk the previous evening. They saw no wrong in what I had done, but I knew that this was what God required of me.

Praise God, I have not drunk any alcohol since, by His grace, and I do not miss it one bit. I am free. Hallelujah.

CHAPTER 19

Because with God nothing is impossible. (Luke 1: 37)

As an eight-year-old, I had had an accident on my bicycle on top of a small hill and grazed my cheek, chipping and fracturing my front tooth. I have had a lot of trouble with my teeth since I was a child. During the period of my parents' separation, we would clean our teeth approximately once a week.

In my mid-forties, I developed a tooth abscess so I had the offending lower molar removed. I was contemplating a root canal, but the pain got too bad and I simply decided it had to go. It turned out to be the correct decision according to the dentist who pulled it out. A couple of years later, the front tooth, which had been injured as a child, also had to go. It had become inflamed. A mould was made of the tooth, and this was made into a plate. It was then discovered that the tooth next to the front tooth had a large filling which had loosened and also needed to be replaced. I proceeded without an injection (I hate needles).

I went home believing that this was the end of it. Instead of the tooth settling down after the dental work (it had not even been sore beforehand), suddenly it became painful. The pain level increased considerably until now the pain was on the scale of a number ten (maximum). This puzzled me, so I rang the dentist. I had been through a lot of dental work, and it had cost Peter a lot of money. The dentist said that sometimes the nerve in a tooth can die due to trauma and that I needed to go and have an X-ray and the new filling would then need to be removed and a root canal put in. This was way more than I could bear, more money and more pain. In desperation, I rang the Joyce Meyer prayer line in Brisbane asking for prayer for my tooth. They gave me the Scripture from Jeremiah 30: 17a which says,

> *'For I will restore health to you, and I will heal you of your wounds, says the Lord.'*

They asked me to confess it out loud to build up my faith. (I had really struggled with declaring my faith verbally in this area.)

Within twenty-four hours, all pain associated with my tooth had completely vanished. Praise God for the victory. I was now completely healed. What I had thought in my limited narrow thinking was that it was too hard even for God. The truth is…

CHAPTER 20

I am leaving peace with you, I give My peace to you: I am giving to you, not just as the world would give. Your heart must not ever trouble you and it must stop being timid. (John 14: 27)

When Rose and I were younger and living with our parents, we grew up knowing that Rose was Mummy's girl and I was Daddy's girl. I guess this tends to happen in a two-child family. I believed that after leaving New Zealand, Rose was paid extra attention. I guess, this was because the adults sympathised with the fact that our mother was no longer a part of the family, and Rose was the younger one. They tried to compensate for her absence.

However, what I did not understand at the time was that my emotions had been overlooked in the process and again, I had not grieved the loss of my mother. As a child, I was completely ignorant of the fact.

One day, as a mature woman in my forties, I watched a television documentary about the life of the actress Natalie Wood and her-then husband Robert Wagner. He spoke about his wife's tragic death from drowning and the effect on their three daughters. Now the interview turned to the two older girls who were now adults. Natalie Wood had died during the middle years of their childhood, which apparently is a vulnerable time. It showed footage of the girls following the coffin down the street at the funeral of their mother. They shared how their mother's premature death and the loss of her presence in their lives had deeply affected them – in fact, it sounded to me as though they were struggling to recover from their grief, *still.*

I ran a bath in our beautiful double spa and poured in some bubble bath to relax. As I sank down into the warm water, I found myself so deeply stirred and moved from what I had just watched on TV because I could so much relate to this true story, the loss of these daughters' mother. I cried from the very depths of my being over the loss of *my own mother* (in different circumstances to theirs but nevertheless, a loss just the same without closure) as a nine-year-old girl whose mother I had left behind all those years ago in Auckland, New Zealand. Mum came over to visit us every couple of years, but that time was emotionally distressing to me as I began to get to know her all over again. There were many unanswered questions of why. Why couldn't I just have a normal mother–daughter relationship like all the other girls? I desperately wanted that, but alas, it was not meant to be. Emotionally, it would have been easier if she had died because then I would have had closure rather than an open emotional wound.

I grieved for about half an hour, and at the end of that time, I had final closure as I accepted the loss of relationship with my mother. God revealed to me that she did the best she could do. I let go of all the expectations I had built up over the years and finally accepted that this was my lot in life. At last, I had peace. Thank you, Lord for your gift of peace.

CHAPTER 21

You will truly tithe all the increase of your seed that the field bring forth year by year. (Deut. 14: 22)

Even though Peter and I attended the apostolic church for some time, we neglected to tithe (to tithe is to give one-tenth of your income back to God, usually to your church). I had felt convicted for some time of the need to tithe but was waiting for my husband to get the revelation.

Eventually, I brought the matter up with him, and he too felt the need to tithe according to what is written in the Word.

The very first Sunday, we tithed, a message was spoken from the pulpit 'that God would bless His people one hundredfold what is tithed as is written in the Word of God.' We put our $50 tithe into the tithing bag which was 10 per cent of Peter's income.

Now the week before, I had purchased some raffle tickets in support of our son's private school. The school had given us a grant for our youngest son to go there. They had given each child a book of tickets to sell over the school holidays which Jethro had not done. I was thankful to the school for what they had done for us, so, even though we found it tight, I purchased ten tickets from the twenty-five-ticket raffle book.

There were two prizes in the offering. First prize was a 4.3 m Savage aluminium boat and trailer with a 10-hp Mercury outboard motor worth a total of $5,000. Second prize was the bookseller's prize which was a mystery flight for the whole family.

One week after tithing, Peter received a phone call. The person on the other end asked Peter if he was sitting down. Peter, not knowing what this was all about, heard the words: 'You have won first prize and in fact second prize as well'. They asked us if we would like to go and pick up our new boat and trailer that afternoon.

Peter rang me straightaway to tell me the exciting news whilst I was visiting a friend. He was overwhelmed by what had just happened and felt unworthy to receive this blessing from God. We were all stunned. Overall, the prizes came to more than a hundredfold although that was not the reason why we tithed. Everything we have and everything we own all comes from God. Ten per cent is such a small amount to return back to him when it all belongs to God. It is so much better to obey what is clearly in the

Word not because we have to, out of a sense of duty, but because we are thankful for all that He has done and given to us.

Thank you, Lord, you are so faithful and gracious. Praise Your Name.

CHAPTER 22

Again I say to you, That if two of you shall agree on earth as touching any thing that they shall ask, it shall be done for them of my Father which is in heaven. For where two or three are gathered together in my name, there am I in the midst of them. (Matt. 18: 19–20, KJV)

I HAD BEEN PRAYING FOR revival. One day, whilst at the supermarket, I was prompted to go and visit a lady called Linda whom I had seen at church. She lived in a little one-bedroom unit on the corner of the main road of Cowes, Phillip Island, Victoria. I called in, shopping in the boot of my car, and stayed for two hours talking about the love we had for God. Our new friendship began. She fascinated me as she operated in the power of the Holy Spirit in a way I had not seen before. Her background had been rough and unusual – she had grown up in Perth, Western Australia, and her father was an electrician. He used to take his young children with him to work before they started school to case the joint. This escalated into a life of crime as an adult, ending up as a heroin addict, and resulting in a jail sentence. She miraculously encountered the Lord there, when a couple of different churches would visit the prisoners. She became a Christian and entered the Teen Challenge program in Perth upon leaving jail. We had powerful prayer times together, and others were drawn to Linda like a magnet from various churches in the area. They were drawn to Holy Spirit in her. Linda had a very kind, caring heart, and everyone felt free and totally safe to talk to her and open up about intimate details of their lives without the fear of being judged.

One afternoon, after calling around, I casually mentioned how, as a Christian, I had struggled in unbelief and had found it hard to fully trust God and His Word. Immediately, Linda got up and said she was going to pray for me. She prayed over me for quite some time, and physically, I began to feel what seemed like electrical currents going up and down my legs. On the drive home, Holy Spirit whispered, 'Now, I can trust you to pray according to my will.'

A house church started up in our home on Sunday mornings and one night mid-week which included our large family and several of my friends, who were mainly single mothers. We were all one big happy family, and we had so much love for one another. We saw God do incredible things, especially among the young people who were attracted to our home church, and for several consecutive days in a row, this person and that person were being baptized including my friend Jeanette and our youngest son Jethro. God answered every *one* of our prayers and this is true. It was amazing. Every time we prayed at night, the lights would flicker, and we *knew* that an angel had been dispatched in answer to every prayer we prayed in Jesus's Name. This was revival. Was I ready for it? I felt overwhelmed at times, and God would remind me that this is what I had prayed for. Some nights, we would pray until the early hours of the morning because we were so excited at what God was doing. We would have prophecies, and one night, my youngest daughter then aged nine had a strong open vision of Jesus standing on green grass. She was in the dining area near the fireplace. We could see that she was physically there, in front of us, but spiritually somewhere else. Another night, my son Grant confessed an area he struggled in and asked for prayer. It was so important to be honest with ourselves and with each other. Praying strongly in Jesus's authority, laying hands on him in the lounge room upstairs, the matter was dealt with. He and the others went outside on the balcony to look at the full moon which now had a halo around it, and I was the only one left in the room. Sitting there quietly, I saw the most brilliant white light shaped in the form of a man come up the stairs and walk around the corner from me and then disappear.

Another time, I laid hands on my husband Peter with Linda on one side and myself on the other when I physically experienced strange symptoms in my body, manifestations, to indicate specifically how to pray for him. I believe that God was taking me to a higher level as God was leading me. It was an incredible season, a time none of us will ever forget. There were not only good times but eventually some not so good, and Peter and I concluded that we needed to have proper training in ministry. It was ultimately a time of character-building, and we were overawed with God.

He is interested in every little detail of our lives and will meet us where our faith is at. As we are available and prepared to step off the cliff for Him by faith in His ability and putting our trust in Him, He will not only meet us where we're at but go way above and beyond our expectation.

END NOTE

We all have a story to tell, the story of our individual lives which, for many people, often consists of heartache and pain and confusion, of brokenness and unanswered questions along the way.

My desire is that my journey would bring hope and encouragement to many, of what the Lord can do in one ordinary woman's life. He is an extraordinary God who loves us and is moved with compassion for us in the midst of our pain. He feels our grief. He is interested in the tiniest details of our lives – nothing is too small for Him. The reason I wrote this book is because our testimony is important. My testimony is about Jesus and what He did for me first of all by dying in my place on the cross.

Revelation 12: 11a says, 'And they overcame him by the blood of the Lamb and by the word of their testimony'. Jesus came to set the captives free, 'He led captivity captive' (Eph. 4: 8).

He went into the very depths of hell to take back the keys, and He paid the ultimate price so we who are lost can be found and pulled out from the hopeless pit called sin. We were born into sin. The only way out is through Jesus Christ and He says that 'I am the way, the truth, and the life: no man comes to the Father, but by me.' (John 14: 6).

God has no favourites. Each one of us is His creation, and just as He loves me, He loves you too. He is a very intimate God and wants intimacy with you, for you to open the door to have that one-on-one relationship with Him. God had been knocking on my heart, and He's knocking on yours too right now.

1 Peter 2: 25 says that 'For you were like sheep going astray; but are now returned to the Shepherd and Bishop of your souls'.

And this is my prayer for you. Return to the One who loves you and cares for you more than the mother or father God has given you. He is your Heavenly Father. Trust Him, believe what the Word of God, the Holy Bible, says, and He will bring it to pass. If you haven't already done so, turn away from a lifestyle of sin, deciding not to travel down that path anymore, and receive the free gift of salvation that Jesus Christ purchased for you through dying on the cross. You were bought at a very high price – Jesus's very own precious blood! Make Him Lord of your life. It may not be easy sailing all the way, but you, like me, will never ever regret the most important, best decision you will ever make. God cares and is in the business of restoring lives. Jesus Christ is the only way. One encounter with Christ will change your life – you will never be the same.

THIS BOOK'S THEME

The word grace is commonly defined as unmerited favour from God alone.

Grace and Mercy are defined as follows:

- Mercy is not getting what you deserve.
- Grace is getting something you don't deserve.

The acumen for the word G. R. A. C. E. is

- God's Righteousness At Christ's Expense
- Grace and Salvation are defined as follows:
- For the grace of God that brings salvation has appeared to all men. (Titus 2: 11, NKJV)

- For by grace you have been saved through faith, and that not of yourselves; *it is* the gift of God, not of works, lest anyone should boast. (Eph. 2: 8–9, NKJV)
- But when the kindness and the love of God our Savior towards man appeared, not by works of righteousness which we have done, but according to His mercy He saved us, through the washing of regeneration and renewing of the Holy Spirit, whom He poured out on us abundantly through Jesus Christ our Savior, that having been justified by His grace we should become heirs according to the hope of eternal life. (Titus 3: 4–7, NKJV)

SALVATION PRAYER

Dear Jesus,

I believe that you are the Son of God and you died upon the cross to take all my sin and wrongdoings. The price you paid for my salvation was with your own blood. You died for me and took my place, and you rose again on the third day. I invite You to come into my life, to fill me and empower me to live for You, God. I make You Lord of my life. I want everything You have for me! I choose to turn away from everything I know to be wrong and fully commit myself to following You because Your ways are good. Thank You, Amen.

Go and tell someone what you have just done and find a group of believers. Your life will be totally changed and things will not be the same as they were. Your friends may decide they no longer want to hang around you any more because your eyes have been opened. Challenges will come but be strong and don't give up. My experience has been I have NEVER regretted the best decision I have made in my life. I pray that this too will be your experience.

When you give yourself, your whole self
to Jesus, He will not let you go!

FURTHER READING

Boundaries by Cloud/Townsend
Set Free by Neil Anderson
Blessings and Curses by Derek Prince
10 Curses that block the blessing by Larry Huch
The Torah Blessing by Larry Huch
Shattering your Strongholds by Liberty Savard
Breaking the Power by Liberty Savard
Producing the Promise by Liberty Savard
Men are from Mars, Women from Venus by John Gray

The following Bible Versions are used in this book:
KJV – King James Version
MSG – Message Version
NKJV – New King James Version.

WEBSITES

www.iregretmyabortion.org.au
www.rachelsvineyard.org
www.opendoors.com.au

www.ingramcontent.com/pod-product-compliance
Lightning Source LLC
LaVergne TN
LVHW010617100826
845148LV00014B/3005

* 9 7 8 0 6 4 8 8 8 7 3 2 4 *